The Fire-Walking Foot Doctor:

One Man's Spiritual Journey

Dr. Rick F. Cohen

The Fire-Walking Foot Doctor:
One Man's Spiritual Journey

Copyright ©2017 Dr. Rick F. Cohen

Book Design by Debbie Ames

Table of Contents

Part One: Sole Currency

Part Two: Soul Currency

This book is dedicated to Anna, my Great Spiritual Teacher and Twin Ray, and to all the Ascended Master Teachers who have once again trusted me to help do their work on this side of the Veil.

I give thanks to my brother Allan for the generous financial and emotional support he has provided, which has allowed me to continue my growth and work in an earnest matter.

The Fire-Walking Foot Doctor

Forward

I have facilitated many Spiritual Workshops throughout the years and many people have asked me if I have a website or if I have written a book. I would always reply with the answer no and never really felt the need to do so.

That all changed the weekend of December 10 and 11 of 2016, as I was invited to address a group of highly successful entrepreneurs out in Los Angeles. The meeting involved people from all over the United States who come to learn new cutting edge technologies and marketing strategies. It was called the Yacht Mastermind Meeting and I was invited to participate and share some spiritual knowledge and meditation techniques with the group.

I was especially motivated by the globally successful life coach and motivational speaker Christopher Kai, who strongly encouraged me to write this book. I also want to thank Jeremy Haynes of Megalodon Digital Marketing Agency for inviting me to speak at this event.

I was so inspired by the energy and integrity of the dynamic men and women I had met. They are doing much to help elevate humanity (especially homeless people and our beloved veterans) that I decided to share my story now in hopes that it may serve as an inspiration to others.

My Spiritual teacher and mentor Anna had always told me that when we do our spiritual teaching and service to others, even if only one individual in the group you are addressing benefits from your efforts then it was still well worth your time and energy.

My hope and intention is that my story will help many, but

as always that is out of my control. I will continue to put all of my heart, compassion and soul into everything I do to be of service to anyone and everyone I can. I hope my experiences will resonate with many, help and inspire and maybe even provide some much needed healing and comfort our world so desperately needs at this time.

And yes, if I have only been able to reach one person through my efforts I will still consider this a success. You know why? Because the way to change this world into a better place is one person at a time.

Introduction

Over the years I have met many people who are on their spiritual path and journeys, this book is about mine.

It is interesting to know that people who are on their quest to explore and find answers to life's many questions usually begin this journey because of some sort of life changing event.

Many people have experienced a traumatic accident or illness in their own lives or to a loved one. Some people have experienced the death of a loved one which started them on the path to search for the deeper meaning of life.

Others have experienced alcohol or drug addiction and have hit rock bottom and look to make sense of their life and how they fit into the bigger picture. Some people have experienced incredible pain and suffering, and, regardless of the circumstances, are just trying to rise above it and somehow find a way, a purpose, a reason to stay alive and feel some happiness.

I believe it all comes down to the basic human premise that we all want and need to be loved as well as to have others to share our love with. When we have this in our lives we feel complete.

This book is divided into two parts. Part One is called "Sole Currency" and refers to our basic day-to-day normal third dimensional existence; more explanation on the unusual title later.

Part Two is called "Soul Currency" and refers to my experiences involving higher dimensions of reality most people are not even aware exist. I know I didn't! I will also include further explanation on choice of this title later.

I hope you enjoy the experiences I was privileged to live through over the years. Allowing oneself to be spontaneous and adventurous creates a whole new outlook on life.

The truth is we never really know what life has waiting for us around the next corner. In my experience it was definitely worth it to pay attention. If we don't keep an open heart and mind, we may miss an amazing opportunity which could easily change the course and quality of our lives.

Dr. Rick Cohen

Part One

Sole Currency

The Fire-Walking Foot Doctor

Chapter One

Life is What Happens
When You are Out Doing Other Things

My story begins on Friday, May 2, 1986 at 2 PM on a Friday afternoon. I was working in my Podiatric medicine and surgery office like any other typical day. My receptionist barged into the exam room and said I was needed on the phone immediately, it was my brother Allan.

I excused myself from my patient and went into my private office to take the call. My father, who had been battling heart disease for many years, was probably the reason for this urgent call. I picked up the phone and my brother was in panic mode. He said dad is in the hospital and things do not look good. You need to get here now!

I hung up the phone, my heart racing, but I still had a few patients to see and had to keep myself in professional mode.

All my medical training and discipline came into play as I finished seeing my patients, and performing a minor procedure on a patient who traveled far to have it done.

I was living in Ohio at the time and had to get to Detroit as soon as possible. My staff got me a reservation on the next available flight.

I then left the office with my heart still racing and a feeling of panic and fear. There was no time to go home and pack, so I drove directly to the airport. After the short flight during which my mind was playing every possible vivid scenario, I jumped in a taxi and headed straight to the hospital.

I arrived at the hospital and went directly to the emergency room, where I met up with my anxious mother and brother. I embraced them both and they told me the doctor had just come out and said my father's condition had stabilized for the time being.

My head was still spinning from all the adrenaline flowing through me, as a couple of hours previously I was having a "normal day".

We had to wait before we were allowed to go in and see him. We decided to get some dinner and were feeling a little better about his prognosis. It appeared my father had dodged a bullet again.

After dinner we were allowed to visit him for a few minutes, then they would transfer him to the Cardiac Intensive Care unit. We knew this routine, as many times over the years he would have relapses and require emergency treatment.

I remembered an incident that had happened while I was still in Podiatry school and home for a visit. At home I noticed he was having difficulty breathing and both his ankles were swollen. Good thing I was paying attention in class the week before when I learned about congestive heart failure and its symptoms.

I knew for certain he was going into congestive heart failure and he needed to get to the hospital immediately! Mom was still at work and I told my father "Your heart is not pumping strong enough and we need to go to the hospital now."

I remember him looking at me with pride in his eyes that I was learning so much in school. He reluctantly agreed with me and off to the hospital we went. It was a good thing we did for I was absolutely correct.

It was after dinner now and we were allowed to visit with him in the emergency room. He saw me immediately and seemed genuinely surprised. "What are you doing here?" he asked?

My father had a good sense of humor (which luckily I inherited from him) and I replied "I heard the cafeteria food here was OFF THE CHARTS GOOD and since I had nothing else planned for this weekend I thought I'd give it a try."

He smiled at my response and said he was feeling fine and that I shouldn't have made the trip. I looked at the color of his face (a good indication of how one's heart is functioning) and he had good color and was making jokes. I knew deep down he was happy to be surrounded by his wife and two sons, and to tell the truth I was happy to be there as well. (Oh, by the way, the cafeteria food was pretty decent as I recall!)

The Fire-Walking Foot Doctor

Chapter Two

Uncle No Film

About ten years prior to my father's most recent heart episode, my brother and I were able to purchase a condo in Boca Raton, Florida for our parents. (Isn't that what all good Jewish sons are supposed to do?)

After my father suffered his second heart attack, my brother and I knew if my parents could spend their winters in Florida it would extend his life. For people with heart conditions, being in a cold winter climate taxes the workload of the heart. We did not want him to have to go through this and were happy to do this for our parents. As it turned out, this absolutely extended his life.

My father's two heart attacks created a dramatic change to my parent's lives; he was also forced into an early retirement at the young age of fifty-four. Dad was an extremely talented and creative men's clothing designer. (No stress there, huh? Having to come up with new patterns and styles four times a year!)

Anyway, getting them this condo in Florida was a new lease on life for both my parents. Not just spending winters in warmer weather, but also the making of new friends. They started actually having some fun again.

Around February of 1986, I decided to go down to Florida and spend a weekend with my parents. I had not seen them in a few months and they always seemed happier and more energetic under the warm Florida sun.

I remember seeing my father's face and I noticed his skin

color had a slight gray tint to it. (Remember me saying the color of the face can reflect the quality of one's heart function?) I did not share this observation with him, but did feel that his life force was becoming noticeably diminished.

During that weekend we shared many stories and jokes, I really enjoyed that time with my parents. I also made sure to take a lot of photographs and have some of them taken of dad and I as well.

I had a great time and made sure to thank my father for all the love and support he had provided to me over the years, even when I was young and reckless. I returned home and felt a heart-to-heart completion with my father, just in case this would be the last time I saw him.

When I returned home, I got my camera out (remember this was way before digital cameras appeared), and to my astonishment and complete surprise there was no film cartridge in the camera. Apparently I had forgotten to check this before I started snapping away. The camera was showing film was in it because after each click a number would appear in increasing value each time I pushed the button. After I realized what I had (or had not!) done, I just started laughing. I could not believe how stupid I had been. The truth is, my connection with my father was far more valuable than a tangible photograph would have been.

As I shared my story with my family and friends, not only did they also find this funny but someone pinned me with the name "Uncle No Film." Even today, many years after the fact, I can still be called this. I have always been able to laugh at myself, and when I think about this incident, it brings a great big smile to my face.

Chapter Three

Life Back in the Cardiac Intensive Care Unit

My family woke up early on Saturday morning, May 3rd, 1986, one day after my father was rushed to the hospital and I had scrambled my way back to Detroit.

We are all feeling positive about my father's newly stabilized condition. After all, he had been through this many times before and had always come through with flying colors. After breakfast, we made our way back to the hospital to see how dad was feeling. Upon entering my father's room, he was in really good spirits and making jokes with us and the nurses. This was typical of his personality and helped lift our spirits as well.

His main nurse entered the room and my father's demeanor changed, and he got real serious for a moment. He started telling the nurse how lucky he was to have such a loving and supportive family and she nodded and smiled right back at him. We were allowed to stay for only a few minutes more and then it was time for him to rest.

I remember one of the doctors told us they were having a hard time regulating his heart rhythm. I was the last to leave his room and remember joking with him about this. He just smiled back at me and made a joke of his own.

We all gathered back in the waiting room area feeling upbeat about his condition. When he was joking and lifting everyone's spirits around him it made us feel that he was going to be fine.

When someone is in cardiac intensive care, visiting time

is generally limited to ten minutes every hour. As we waited for another hour to pass, we heard over the intercom those dreaded words "Code Blue" (Code Blue means a patient is in cardiac arrest), a definite life and death situation.

We heard nurses and doctors scrambling about. We never thought for a moment that our father was involved because just minutes earlier we were in his room making jokes with him.

A few agonizing moments later, we were told our father had expired. Words cannot express the feelings going on within me then. The shock we all felt was overwhelming. How could this happen when a few minutes earlier he was laughing and bragging to his nurse how lucky he was to have such a loving family?

This whole experience was very surreal, it's as if time had stopped, and everyone was speaking and moving in slow motion. I thought of my mother's pain and held her to try and comfort her. We were all crying uncontrollably, still in disbelief.

My father's main nurse came to talk with us. She told us how nice it had been to meet and take care of our father, and how nice he was. Her words were very comforting, God bless her for that. As we started to accept the reality of his passing, she said we could go back in his room in a few minutes and say goodbye. I will never forget walking in that room seeing his body lying in the bed, his face totally gray now and lifeless.

I bent over and kissed him goodbye on the lips, and I will never forget how cold they felt. There was no room for denial here, as this definitely proved he had passed away.

Chapter Four

Sense of Loss and the Funeral

I remember immediately leaving the hospital with a sense of disbelief, shock and an overwhelming feeling of sadness. I knew my life would never be the same again.

In the Jewish tradition funerals are done quickly so decisions and arrangements were made rapidly. It is amazing how in such a raw emotional state one can find the ability to focus and accomplish much in such a short period of time. In other words, no matter what is going on in your life, you do what you have to do.

Later that evening at my parent's house, friends and family started stopping by to offer their love and support. It is amazing how powerful Love can be at a time like this.

I have later come to realize that grieving is a very personal process and that everyone has the right to grieve in whatever way they choose, without being judged.

When I experienced this grief, I had no spiritual knowledge or foundation to help me. All I knew was how incredibly sad, fragile and alone I felt. I started a relationship with my new best friend (at least for the next few days) a Mr. Chivas Regal. For those not familiar with this name, it is a popular brand of scotch whiskey. I was never a big drinker but a few shots of this stuff helped to numb my pain, at least temporarily.

Again, as I sat in my parent's living room while people came over to offer their kind words and comfort, I could not stop thinking how surreal this all seemed. I had attended the homes of people who had lost loved ones to offer my support, and now I was on the receiving end.

It was now the day of the funeral, and I am glad we decided to do it in the morning. It was best to put this day behind us as rapidly as possible because the pain was unbearable.

The funeral seemed to fly by in my mind, and I do not really remember much about it. I remember seeing many friends and family and appreciated them being there to not only honor my father's life but ours as well.

After the funeral, we arrived back at my parent's house somewhat relieved that we got through it. I needed some alone time and headed to the family room at the back of the house.

I had just started looking out the large glass sliding door, out into the backyard and noticed a large black bird sitting on a telephone wire connected to the house. My eyes then locked onto the eyes of this bird for what felt like a really long time. As I continued to be fixated on the eyes of this bird, all of a sudden I heard my father's voice as clear as day. He said, "DON'T WORRY ABOUT ME, I'M OKAY!!!" Now before I continue, let me tell you I had in no way spent any time with my friend Mr. Chivas Regal on this day, at least not yet!

When I first heard my father's voice and the message, I felt a warm sensation from the top of my head to the bottom of my feet. For an instant I felt a strong and real reconnection with dad, and was no longer worried about him.

Curious, you better believe it!

Confused, you better believe it!

The sense of calmness and relief I experienced is hard to describe. The fact that whatever form he was in now was still able to communicate with me was priceless; unbelievable, but priceless nonetheless.

Now I thought, what should I do with this experience? Do

I dare share it with my family (who already think I'm a little different and crazy anyway) or do I keep it to myself until I can totally wrap my head around what just happened?

I decided to keep this moment private at this time for fear of waking up in a rubber room under lock and key. Truth is, it wasn't until years later that I shared the story to anyone I knew personally.

The Fire-Walking Foot Doctor

Chapter Five

Now What?

In a few days it was time for me to return to Ohio and go back to work. Upon returning home I found myself thinking a lot about my father and my experience with him in the family room after his funeral. I had so many questions, but the feeling of his message still resonated deep within my heart. Here I was, 29 years old with four successful podiatric medical practices, living what I thought was the American dream (whatever that is). The truth was, I felt totally lost, confused and in need of some answers to life's questions, such as:

What happens to us after we die?

Why are we here in the first place?

What is our purpose?

Is there a much bigger picture here than
we are aware of?

On a personal note I wanted to know:

Why am I here?

What is my purpose?

Will I ever feel whole again?

Those were just some of the questions that came up for me. I felt so empty you could have driven a big MACK truck right through my soul! I will tell you this, I was determined to get some answers and so I began my journey on my spiritual quest and path.

Many truthseekers I have encountered over the years share a familiar life-altering event which causes them to look at life differently.

Some have experienced the loss of a loved one, others have been in serious accidents, others have gone through life threatening illnesses and diseases, while others may have hit rock bottom due to drug or alcohol dependency. Others have had to face extreme dramatic life experiences physically, mentally, emotionally, and even all three at the same time.

My father would often tell me if everyone was to hang all their problems on a clothesline and after looking around at other people's problems, more times than not you would choose to hang onto your own.

He also used to say that every day you read the paper and your name is **not** in the obituary column is a good day! (This is another example of his sense of humor thrown in with a life lesson.)

Dr. Rick Cohen

Chapter Six

My Neighborhood Corner Metaphysical Bookstore

One day while driving down the street in my small town, I passed a small storefront and the sign read "Metaphysical Bookstore." Not knowing what a metaphysical bookstore was, I stopped in to find out. Inside was a very kind, compassionate woman who happened to own the store as well. My first question for her was, "What does the term metaphysical mean?" She explained it refers to things in life that are "more than physical," spiritual things both seen and unseen.

I felt very comfortable in her presence and shared with her the story about my father's passing. I finally shared with another human being my father's post funeral message. As she listened intently, she was totally open and nonjudgmental to my story. She then smiled at me, saying what a blessing it was for both me and my father that I was open enough to receive his message.

I thought, what does she mean when she says I was "open enough?" I did not pursue that thought any further that day, but told her I needed to find some answers and could she recommend some books to help get me started?

The time frame for this encounter was some 30 years ago, and I cannot remember the specific books she recommended for me so long ago. What I can tell you is I have since read hundreds of books, attended many spiritual conferences and have never stopped my quest for higher truth. Yes, I have learned much and I will share a lot of that with you in the coming pages. The absolute truth is, no matter what your

27

calling in life may be, the more you learn the more you realize you don't know. So let's continue on this journey to learn more together, and all I ask is that you keep an open mind.

As the months went by, I continued to go through large quantities of books in search of answers. One day I got a call from my friend David inviting me to join him out west in Taos, New Mexico for what he said was a self-empowerment conference led by a man named Stuart Wilde.

This conference was all about taking you out of your comfort zone and allowing a safe, controlled way of facing your fears. Some of the events being offered were a high ropes challenge course, repelling off the side of a mountain, spending the night out on a mountain by yourself, and concluding with a fire walk, just to mention a few of the events.

Yes, you heard me, the week would end with the infamous walking over hot coals. Now here I am in my thirties, a practicing podiatric surgeon, thinking about doing all these things including walking over hot coals. Was I crazy? Yes, maybe a little, but I agreed to go do this event for reasons I would not totally understand until a few years later.

Let me review here, I do not like heights; I found out later there was a meditation involving snakes and I definitely do not like snakes; and lastly, I never heard of anyone crazy enough to walk over hot coals. Wow, I thought, what a perfect way to spend five days!

Dr. Rick Cohen

Chapter Seven

Time to Put My Feet to the Fire, Literally!!

I arrived in Taos, New Mexico in the spring of 1988 ready to participate in a five-day self empowerment seminar (whatever that meant).

There were a total of 150 participants from all walks of life attending this event. This was my first spiritual conference and I had no idea what to expect. Many of the people I met had already dropped out of the rat race to pursue their spiritual interests. Here I was, totally entrenched into my third dimensional life with the responsibility of four podiatric medical offices. I had also met people who claimed to be healers, psychics and all varieties of new age practitioners. I pretty much felt like a fish out of water but didn't care, I was here for new experiences.

As the conference started, we were immediately broken up into smaller groups for the purpose of doing different events simultaneously. There were 15 people in our group, One of the women was from Durango, Colorado, a connection that would later prove to have a significant influence on my life.

As the events began to unfold, we started on a high ropes challenge course with one of the stations involving climbing straight up a tree about thirty feet high. Once at the top we were to stand on a small platform and for no apparent reason, take a flying lunge (Leap of Faith) off the top. We were secured by ropes and harnesses that prevented us from jumping to our death, but it did take a real sense and surge of courage to do it anyway.

29

Seeing as heights has never been one of my favorite things, I made sure to volunteer to go first. I figured that way my anxiety would not have an opportunity to overwhelm me and I would not have to witness other people's fears and insecurities either.

I remember climbing up the small wood blocks attached on either side of the tree, my legs slightly shaking from the fear. I pushed upward regardless of the fear and reached the top where a one-foot square wooden platform was located. As I found my balance, I was now standing straight up on the small platform and felt adrenaline rushing through my veins as well as my heart pounding. There was a bar that appeared to be about five feet in front of me suspended by another rope. The purpose of this bar was to be a focal point to aim for and grab as you jumped. (I later found out it was purposely placed so you could not reach it, but it did provide your ego a reason and challenge to jump.)

After taking a deep breath, and with a lot of encouragement from my group down below, I sprung off that platform falling short of the bar, but was gently and safely lowered to the ground. Wow! I am still alive! What a rush! Everyone came up and hugged me and I felt like I could conquer the world.

So this is what self-empowerment feels like, I like it!!! The first experience for me was exhilarating and empowering at the same time. All my bones and psyche were still intact. So far so good I thought.

The next day we sat on the floor in the conference hall and were put into a deep meditative state of relaxation. Without any prior warning ,staff members began placing snakes (that's right, you heard me!) over different parts of our bodies. Although we were in this deep state of relaxation, you could still feel the snakes slither and crawl over your arms, legs, neck and head. Did I mention I hate snakes!!

I began doing more deep breathing and to this day I cannot believe how calm I was during this exercise. Under other circumstances my heart would have been pounding right through my chest, but not on this day, my friends. On this day I was in total control of my emotions. (Well, I like to think so anyway.)

We knew going into this conference that we were in a controlled environment for the most part and had to trust the people in charge. We knew the snakes were not poisonous although the fear factor was still real. If I ever encounter a snake in the wild, I promise you I have no intention to just sit and start breathing so it can crawl all over me. I am **no**t quite ready to do my Tarzan impression yet, but I am closer to it than if I had never had this experience.

That evening it was time to spend the night on the mountain by ourselves. I remember it was cold and completely pitch black. Animals could be heard scurrying around. No fear, anxiety or trepidation here!!

As we were driven up the mountain, we were dropped off one by one and told to walk at least 100 yards in from the road and find a comfortable spot to sit.

As I began walking into the dense forested area, my eyes adjusted to the dark just enough for me to find a soft spot and take a seat.

I heard the sound of a gently flowing stream in the distance, which was somewhat comforting until I also heard some animals splashing through the water. Here I was on a mountain in the middle of nowhere, surrounded by animals and nature, it was cold and dark and probably more dangerous than I wanted to admit (maybe now was the time to think about changing travel agents!!) Initially I felt a little anxious but started doing some deep breathing and eventually realized I was a guest on this mountain.

I surrendered to the energy of the mountain and the animals and asked if I could remain here for a while totally safe and protected. I learned to do this from a Native American Guide who taught us to have great respect and reverence of Mother Earth and Mother Nature. As soon as I remembered to do this, I felt a deep sense of inner peace, relaxation and knew I was completely safe.

The hours flew by and I felt my energy melt into the mountain as I became one with nature. Before I knew it I saw the lights from the van in the distance. Someone got out and called for us to come off the mountain. Soon we were back at the hotel enjoying hot soup and sharing our stories with the others.

Again, as in other challenges I faced this week, it appears that surrendering to fear makes it easier to overcome.

If we fuel our fear it just becomes worse, if we learn to breath through it and relax we are able to function more efficiently. (NEVER UNDERESTIMATE THE POWER OF DEEP BREATHING.) As the week continued, I felt I was gaining some inner momentum which I could take with me and use in my day-to-day life.

The next day we experienced a Native American Sweat Lodge Ceremony. This takes place in an igloo shaped dome made of tree branches covered with blankets. At the center of the floor is a fire pit designed to hold multiple extremely hot lava rocks. A fire is built outside the structure and is used for heating the lava rocks.

For Native Americans this is a very sacred cleansing ritual. Initially you enter in as a group sitting in circular fashion. One by one the hot rocks are brought into the center and placed in the pit. As more and more rocks are added, the heat becomes extreme and it feels as if there is no air to breathe.

I quickly figured out if I surrendered to the heat and just stared into the glow of the hot rocks I could relax and benefit from the spiritual and physical cleansing. It was a very intense experience and afterwards I felt much lighter. I was extremely relaxed and proud that I was able to overcome some claustrophobia as well.

So far so good, I thought. I had been handling whatever they threw in my direction and my sense of confidence and power seemed to expand and grow hourly. One of the lessons learned seem to be that in order for one to grow, one needs to leave their comfort zone. It is also interesting to note that each one of us has their own unique comfort zone which we create for ourselves to make us feel safe, secure and comfortable.

So far this experience has proven invaluable for me and made me realize that we are never too old for change or even to experience new challenges and breakthroughs.

Up until then I had enjoyed the challenges, the many interesting people I met, and the pure adrenaline rush from breaking through some of my own fears. Tomorrow night however would be the final exam! Walking across hot coals.

So here we are on the last day of this amazing week, which will be topped off by the evening's fire-walking event. I admit during the whole day I felt like I had a pit of pure fear and anxiety building up in my stomach.

After all, what was there to be afraid of? I only had eight years of college that taught me walking on hot coals can never be a good thing. I had been practicing podiatric medicine and surgery for about six years now and my training and experience dictated that exposing the bottom of your feet to extreme temperatures (on purpose) is pure insanity!!!!

Well, I had come this far and certainly had no intention of not finishing this out. It was about 5pm and we all met outside in the back parking lot of the hotel for the official lighting of the bonfire. This wood fire would eventually become the hot coals we were to walk across later that evening. It was the biggest, most dramatic intense bonfire I had ever seen. If the intent of those in charge of this was to scare the crap out of everyone and produce mass quantities of anxiety, I would say mission accomplished!!

We were then instructed to go eat dinner but remain silent and contemplate the evening fire walk. After dinner (like anyone could really have an appetite), we met back in the conference hall waiting for the sun to go down. (Walking HOT COALS at night with their glowing red embers makes it much more dramatic, doesn't it?)

The tension in the room was palpable. It was interesting the crazy thoughts ego can come up with when we are under extreme stress. We were put into a deep meditative state and this time we were led into a visualization as we saw ourselves walking across the hot coals with no problem. This turned out to be a very powerful way of overcoming fear. If you have something in your life to do that is stressful, try some deep breathing and then visualize yourself doing it perfectly.

It was now time to go outside, and we all lined up single file. You could have heard a pin drop if only your own heart wasn't beating so loud and fast. Once outside, we were organized by groups and it was time to get this party started.

Group after group began lining up in front of the HOT COALS and took their turn walking across. The energy of the whole group began to increase as everyone was encouraging each other to just do it! As best as I could tell, no one had experienced a spontaneous combustion of the physical form on their journey across the COALS, so maybe there was a method to this madness. It was now my turn to walk. As I approached the HOT GLOWING COALS I took a deep breath in and then exhaled slowly, and then calmly walked across to the other side. As I finished it felt surreal to me, almost as if I left my body during this experience. All my body parts were still intact, especially my feet. I felt no discomfort whatsoever. Once I reached the other side I immediately looked back at the hot coals, as my ego was in total denial of what I had just done and tried to invalidate it in my mind.

I would show my ego who's boss here, so I immediately got back in line and walked again. Take that EGO!! You're not the boss of me!!

Doing this firewalk was one of the most exciting and adrenaline-producing experiences of my life. I had never felt so alive!!

So here is the secret challenge in doing a fire walk: the hot coals are a metaphor of whatever fears or obstacles you're currently facing in your life. By mustering all your courage to take that first step, you are proving to yourself on some level you have the courage to overcome any future challenge in your life. By the way, the first step is the most difficult. After that your survival mode kicks in and getting across to the other side is easy. This proved to be an amazing self-empowerment exercise. You surely take from this experience inspiration, self-confidence, and empowerment to believe you can NOW do anything in your life.

Okay, so let's get back to all my scientific and medical training, which taught me you should not be able to do this without getting injured. This experience taught me firsthand the Power of our Mind, (the Power of positive thinking and visualization) and the Power of our Intention (focus and will). Since this experience I have walked hot coals numerous times and only got burned one time. I was walking in front of some friends, my ego got involved, I lost my focus and suffered slight blistering on the bottom of one foot. Thank you God, lesson learned!

Another big thing I took away from my initial firewalking experience was to start questioning everything and no longer simply accept third dimensional reality as the be all and end all of Total Truth. If focusing our mind can allow us to walk across hot coals safely, what else might be possible? I now felt that science was not fool- proof and just because you were led to believe certain facts doesn't necessarily make them 100% accurate.

As a side note, a few years later I took a course to become a Certified Firewalking Instructor. (Yes, there is such a thing! Don't you just love Californians?)

I have now walked well over a hundred times and still live to tell my story. By the way, is there a better business model for building up a podiatric medical practice than to host a free neighborhood fire walk? Just think of all the new patients you would acquire after they burned their feet.

Just saying! (I am kidding, or am I ???)

In closing, if you ever find yourself in a rut, I definitely recommend you get out of your comfort zone. Go try something new, adventurous, or totally out-of-the-box. It will truly make you feel alive! You deserve to be happy, so what are you waiting for?

Chapter Eight

Do You Believe In Spirits? (Say What?)

I returned to Ohio after my New Mexico trip a newly revitalized and empowered person. My energy was off the charts and I had to learn to dial it down and return to my routine of seeing and treating my patients (easier said than done). I could not stop thinking about all the amazing things I had experienced in Taos and all the interesting people.

I had never met so many people living on the fringe of society, just being on their spiritual path and living one day at a time. This concept was foreign to me as I went from high school, to college, to podiatry school, to my surgical residency, and then to work. The idea of taking time off just to be was something I had never even considered.

While in New Mexico, we would get up at 4 a.m. every morning for a group meditation. It was explained to us that getting up this early made it easier to concentrate and focus on the meditation. With most people still sleeping, there were less thought patterns in the atmosphere to contend with. I had never really thought about this before but it appeared to make sense, so I went along with the program.

Upon returning home, I continued the practice of getting up at 4 a.m. to meditate, much to my girlfriend's surprise and confusion.

One morning I woke up just like any other day at 4am and did my meditation in my living room as I always had. When I finished it was still dark and I decided to go outside to look at the stars and get some fresh air. Off the back of my house was a tiered three-level deck overlooking a small lake. The top level was off the living room, the middle level had a large table and chairs, and the bottom level had a self-contained Jacuzzi.

As I walked out my living room door onto the deck, I noticed the night sky full of stars and that the air had a cool bite to it. I was still in a relaxed state of mind following my meditation until I looked to my left, and to my astonishment, saw the figure of a man wearing a long white robe sitting at the table on the mid-level deck just smiling at me. He had long white hair and matching beard and appeared to be totally illuminated in blazing white light. My initial reaction was one of total disbelief, my second was one of total panic. (So much for all my self-empowerment training, right?)

I immediately ran back into the house, my heart racing. I totally freaked out and the only thing I could think of was to hurry up and lock the door behind me. (Where was that brave warrior dude who triumphantly walked across the hot coals barely a week ago now?)

At that moment I no longer felt like Superman, but felt like stupor-man instead. Why was I so afraid? And who was this individual bathed in magnificent white light? One thing for sure, he certainly wasn't a third dimensional human being. The answers to these questions came to me further down the road in time, but at least I finally did get an explanation. (How is that for a teaser to encourage you to keep reading?)

After I ran back into the house and locked the door behind me, you know what the first thought that popped into my head was? I thought what an idiot I am. This Being of Light, whoever he was, could just as easily walked right through the walls to get in if he so desired.

After my heart rate returned to normal, I sat alone in the dark trying to make sense of what just happened. (And yes, I

38

kept looking out the window to see if he was still there but no he was gone.)

Life is interesting, just when you think you have things all figured out something like this happens and you feel like it's back to square one.

I again had an unbelievable experience that defied third dimensional logic, and what was I supposed to do with it? I decided not to share this with anyone until years later, who would have believed me anyway? I remember I had read that there were Advanced Souls, sometimes referred to as "ASCENDED MASTERS," who have the ability to materialize whenever and wherever they choose. Is that what happened here? Had I been visited by one of my Spiritual Guides who resides in a higher dimension of reality?

Many traditions teach that there are twelve dimensions of existence or reality. If we as conscious human beings reside in the third dimension what exists in the other nine? Without giving too much of my story away, I was told years later that this individual was in fact one of my Spirit Guides and that he came to introduce himself to me and give me a message to help guide me in my future decisions. I have since learned we all have them, regardless of our belief system.

Obviously at that point I was not strong enough or willing enough to face him and hear what he had to tell me (I have my ego to thank for that). Believe me when I tell you I wish I had. I now know what he was trying to teach me, but at that time wanted no part of it. If I had stayed outside and communicated with him, I may have made different choices and saved myself going through some unnecessary emotional drama and trauma in my personal life, at the same time also saving money, energy, and time. It is what it is, and this proved to be a valuable lesson for me. These Spirit Guides have to respect our individual free fill and for the most part cannot interfere. However, they are constantly working behind the scenes on our behalf trying to help us and push us in the right direction for our own Soul's growth.

If something like this should ever happen to you, please learn from my mistake and definitely have the courage to accept what I later found out was a true Blessing from God.

Chapter Nine

New Ending and Newer Beginnings

After my experience of seeing a materialized Being of Light, I was more determined than ever to read more, to learn more about the Higher Spiritual Truths of Life. I continued to plow through many books looking for more answers. Truth is I wasn't even sure what the questions were. As I continued on my spiritual quest and still kept my day job of treating patients, a deep feeling of restlessness was emerging from inside me.

It was now about three years after my experience (or lack thereof) on my back deck, and I realized it was time for a change.

I decided to sell my medical offices and my house, and relocated to Florida with my girlfriend. I thought a change of scenery would be beneficial for both of us. (You know, the grass is always greener type of thing.)

Well, once again I couldn't have been more wrong. After a short-lived marriage, and me not enjoying my new work experience, I knew it was time for some major changes.

My life was no longer working for me, I was not happy. My life up till now was very scripted. I had gone to college for eight years, done a one-year surgical residency, and then 10 years at private practice. It was now January, 1992, six years since my father's death and I still had no inner peace. I kept thinking about some of the people I met in Taos in 1988, and how they shared stories of selling all their stuff and just traveling around the world.

This all sounded very tempting to me. I was still young, only 36 years old at the time, and my soul was bursting at the seams to have fun and, more importantly, continue my spiritual quest for truth and enlightenment. Did I have the courage to drop out of the rat race?

I took some time to think about my father, and some of the spiritual experiences I had had since he was gone. I wondered what else was out there for me to discover. One thing I knew for sure, it felt like my life had hit rock bottom and something needed to change for me. I was unhappy, tired of failed relationships, and there was a deep driving force within me to just go for it. I had a decent amount of money put away in the bank, so what was I afraid of?

For the second time in my life (the first walking on hot coals for the first time) I decided to go against the grain of all common sense and made the decision to quit practicing medicine, to put my belongings in storage, put on a backpack and begin my wonderful adventure of a lifetime!

When I finally shared my decision with close friends and family, they all thought I was crazy and gave me a million reasons why I couldn't or shouldn't do this.

I was determined and stuck to my guns. I later realized that making such a major decision in my life was bringing up other people's fears and insecurities as well.

My plan was to travel around the world for one year and then deal with the rest of my life after that. I saw this as a great opportunity to do some real soul-searching and learn who I was and what my life's purpose was. It was time for me to step out from wearing my white doctor's coat and learn my true identity. Back then, if you asked me who I was, I would have replied 'I am a doctor.' In reality that is not who I am, but just one of the many roles I play, being a doctor was a career choice. Just think how many of us define ourselves by our jobs, our roles (mother, father, husband, wife, brother, sister, friend, etc.)

I wanted to dig deeper to find out who I really am, and how I fit in to the bigger picture we call LIFE!

The Fire-Walking Foot Doctor

Chapter Ten

What is Sole Currency Anyway?

This book is divided into two parts. Part One is titled Sole Currency and I wanted to explain what I mean by this. Since I made my living up until 1992 working as a doctor on people's feet, this title refers to that part of my life when sole currency represented my third dimensional currency income produced by working on people soles! (A play on words, for sure.)

Up to this point, my life was firmly entrenched in the rat race of bills, responsibilities, stress and the collecting of material possessions. Sound familiar to anyone?

It was now time for me to get out from under all this stuff and see what I could see, learn what I could learn, and definitely experience new places, people, and things.

As a side note, my one-year plan of adventuring is now going on twenty-five years and not one day goes by that I am not learning something new about myself or others.

Remember what I learned in Taos, New Mexico? How sometime you have to leave your comfort zone to grow? With that in mind, let's get extremely uncomfortable and get this party started!!!

The Fire-Walking Foot Doctor

Part Two

Soul Currency

The Fire-Walking Foot Doctor

Chapter One

My Spiritual Journey Begins

As previously stated in part one of this book, I decided to drop out of the "Rat Race" to embark on a year long spiritual backpacking adventure around the world by myself. Before I left, I decided to spend a couple of months out west in Albuquerque, New Mexico with some friends I met years earlier at a self-empowerment conference back in 1988. I was still living in South Florida at the time and thought driving out west and staying for awhile would help clear my head and better prepare me for my around-the-world trek. It was now the summer of 1992 and my plan was to return to Florida in August and then begin my international itinerary in September sometime after Labor Day.

In addition to spending time in New Mexico, I had made plans to visit another friend in Durango, Colorado, a short four-hour drive away. Remember me telling you about a woman I had met in Taos who was in my group at the self empowerment conference years earlier? Well, she was living in Durango and her name is Pam (much more on this later).

Arriving in New Mexico, I enjoyed my reconnection with my friends Susan and C.G. (yes, he only went by these initials). I shared with them that for a long time I had been dealing with low energy and feeling tired most of the time. I had blood work taken before heading out west and everything was normal, except the way I was feeling physically. They recommended a local doctor they knew and I immediately made an appointment, hoping for a quick diagnosis and cure. By the way, I want you to know that us doctors make the worst patients.

When I arrived for my appointment and finished filling out the forms, I had a long list of symptoms on it, and before I even saw the doctor they requested I give a blood sample. A few minutes later they led me into a room where the doctor was looking at a slide of my blood under a microscope. He said come here, I want you to see what the problem is. As I looked through the microscope he explained there were yeast cells floating around in my bloodstream producing toxins and causing me to feel tired all the time. I could actually see them moving around and my initial reaction was, thank God I am not crazy after all, there was in fact a physical cause for my symptoms.

He said I was suffering from a chronic yeast infection originating in my stomach. With my medical history of many previous sinus infections and overuse of antibiotics I had developed an imbalance of bacteria in my stomach. Antibiotics not only kill bad bacteria but they can also kill good bacteria, which our bodies need to maintain our health and balance. It is now believed that a strong immune system in our bodies starts with a healthy, balanced bacteria count in our stomach. In my case, because of taking many courses of antibiotics over time, my intestinal and stomach bacteria were way out of balance, allowing these yeast cells to multiply with no resistance and thereby producing toxins.

With my medical background I had always associated yeast infections in women not men. I had been to doctors before and not one of them ever thought to consider this diagnosis. I cannot tell you how relieved I was to know there was a physical cause for my symptoms. He explained that when these toxins get into the blood stream they totally compromise the immune system causing all kinds of issues.

He assured me this was easily treatable but would require some discipline on my part, at least initially. He prescribed a regimen of anti-fungal pills, a very strict diet, and then something I had never heard of before called Ayurvedic medicine, based on Eastern Indian medicine which promotes balance not only physically but spiritually as well. It dates back almost 3000 years and at this point I was open to trying anything. I left the office thrilled that there was now a cure in sight and looked forward to receiving some Ayurvedic treatment as well.

I have included my experience about my candida (the specific name of the yeast) infection here because many people today are diagnosed under the broad heading "Chronic Fatigue Syndrome," when doctors have no other reasonable diagnosis to offer. My hope is that maybe some of those people have what I had and can be helped.

There is an excellent book called *The Yeast Connection: A medical breakthrough* by William G. Crook. If you know someone who has Chronic Fatigue, headaches, muscle pain, etc. maybe this book can help.

My whole life is now based on being of service to others, as you will learn as my story progresses. Even if only one person benefits from my sharing of this information, I feel as if I've done my job.

The Fire-Walking Foot Doctor

Chapter Two

My Pancha-Karma Experience (My What!?)

I signed up for an Ayurvedic treatment called Pancha-Karma, a process used to help detox the body as well as re-align the mental, emotional and spiritual aspects of ourselves. At this point I had no knowledge or experience with Ayurvedic medicine, but was totally open to anything that could rebalance my body and help heal me.

I arrived for my appointment to undergo this Pancha-Karma treatment (still not knowing what is was) strongly recommended to me by a nurse at the doctor's office where I had received my diagnosis. This was my first experience of any type of "Alternative Medicine", and immediately upon entering the clinic felt peaceful and calm. Relaxing music was playing in the background, the lighting was dimmed and the smell of burning incense filled the air. I guess this is what non-traditional medical clinics are like. I did not know for sure but it did feel good to be here.

As I entered my treatment room, I observed a large table in the corner similar to a massage bed. The room was dimly lit and there were candles lit throughout. I still had no idea what was in store for me but was still feeling totally calm and relaxed.

A young woman walked into the room explaining she would be giving the treatment today and did I have any questions. I told her this was my first experience in Ayurvedic medicine and had no idea what to expect. She explained the Pancha-Karma treatment involves the use of a continuous stream of hot oil directed over the center of the forehead (also referred to as the Pineal Gland). I would later learn that in spiritual circles the center of the forehead is also referred to as the "third eye." It is believed when this area of the brain is activated it opens us up to higher spiritual frequencies and dimensions of truth and experience. (At this point in time I did not know or understand any of this, I just wanted to feel better, plain and simple!)

As I continued to listen to her explanation, I kind of spaced out to the rest of the details and was anxious to begin. She then left the room while I undressed and laid on my back under the sheet on the table. She re-entered the room, and placed a clear plastic tarp all around me and under my head and neck in order to catch the oil as it flowed off my forehead.

She then instructed me to close my eyes and just relax. I began to feel a light stream of hot oil gently hitting the center of my forehead. It was a strange sensation but at the same time the hot oil felt very soothing as I became more and more relaxed. After a while I felt myself beginning to gently float out of my body with a deep sense of peace and relaxation. I had never felt anything like this before and I liked it. I felt totally light and free. I lost all sense of time. I was experiencing this state of bliss for what seemed like an eternity. I then found myself in a room unlike anything I had ever seen before.

There I was, lying on a table in the center of this room surrounded by chairs with risers like you might find in an amphitheater. I was at the bottom of this room with theater type chairs surrounding me on all sides. It reminded me of the old time surgical operatory theaters where doctors would come to look down and observe operations being performed. I felt like I was the one to be observed today.

I sat up and looked around and at first all I could see

were individual beams of light filling up the seats. As my eyes adjusted, I began to see the outlines of individual bodies and faces both male and female. Where was I? And who were these Beings of Light? I knew for sure I wasn't in Kansas anymore (sorry for the much overused Wizard of Oz reference), but I was still totally at peace. As I continued to look around the room I noticed at the far end was a raised bench like you would find in a courtroom where the judge would sit. In this case there were three individuals sitting behind this elevated bench, overseeing all the other Beings of Light and I.

I then heard a voice from someone in the theater seats say, "What is he doing here, he is not dead yet?" I thought to myself, wait, say what? Where was I? And why am I here? Surely I'm not dead! Or am I?

One of the three individuals behind the bench stood up and started to address the group. I knew by the robe he was wearing and the authority in his voice that he was in a position of power higher than the others in the room.

He first addressed the group by saying yes, this is a situation usually reserved for humans who have physically died and crossed over back to the spirit world, but today is different.

I was still somewhat confused and then he addressed me directly. He said the place you now find yourself in is a place where Souls go once they have left Earth after each lifetime. They are brought here so we can review their life with them. This process is a loving one, not a judgmental one and serves as a learning and teaching opportunity to further advance their soul's growth. Once they leave here they are taken to a different dimension to continue their training until it is time for them to once again return to Earth and inhabit another physical form.

Then, as if he was reading my mind, he continued: "You

were brought here today out of your body as a blessing for you, that you would learn and understand firsthand that the Soul is Immortal. At the end of each human embodiment you are evaluated, not judged, on your Soul's performance of being of service to others and in helping raise humanity. You were allowed to come here today and see behind the veil because you have important work to do in this lifetime. What you have seen and learned today will serve to inspire and encourage you as you go forward into your new life."

I immediately felt so blessed and honored to be in the presence of such loving, majestic, and wise Beings of Light. Who was I to be receiving such a blessed gift?

The next thing I heard was the therapist's gentle voice telling me the session was over. She advised me to take my time getting off the table before getting dressed. I didn't want this experience to end, but gradually got up and reluctantly returned to third dimensional planet Earth.

It's interesting for me as I am writing these words, because I once again feel the same loving energy as I did 25 years ago. These Beings of Light are real (I know because I have now seen them twice, once in my body, and now once out of my body). Just because you can't see them or don't believe in them, doesn't mean they don't exist and are not helping humanity behind the scenes at this time (much more on this later).

After leaving the clinic and driving back to my friend's house, I felt totally blissed out by my experience. I don't know how this "Pancha-Karma" therapy was supposed to heal my physical body but the rest of me felt blessed, honored and a deep inner peace. I would no longer fear death, but embrace life with a new energy and drive. I wanted to learn more, so one day I would be in a position to help others, and maybe even humanity as a whole. I had no idea what important work I was supposed to do in the future, but I became excited just thinking about it. You better believe I was going to share this experience with my friends. After all they too were on their spiritual path and would not dismiss me as being crazy. If you ever have the chance to have a Pancha Karma treatment where you live, I absolutely recommend you try it. Who knows what may happen for you?

Back at my friend's house, I thought wow! I have not even left the United States yet and look what I just got to experience. This was further validation that I made the right choice in leaving my old life behind. I could not wait for what I would see, learn and do next. For now I would just settle for a good night's sleep.

While still in New Mexico, my friends recommended I schedule an astrological reading with a man up in Santa Fe, about an hour's drive north of Albuquerque. I booked my appointment and thought this would be an interesting experience. However it was not the life-altering enlightenment I was hoping for. He did tell me about an upcoming event in Santa Fe, featuring a woman known as the "Hugging Saint." She was a Hindu spiritual leader and he strongly recommended that I attend this event.

I returned to Albuquerque and made arrangements to visit my friend Pam up in Durango, Colorado. I had met Pam at a self-empowerment event years earlier and she invited me to stay with her if I was ever in the area. She told me about a friend of hers named Anna who did psychic readings for people, taught meditation classes and facilitated rebirthing sessions.(whatever that meant!).

I made sure my trip up to Durango lined up with the meeting in Santa Fe with the "Hugging Saint." After all, this was on my way to Durango and I was more than a bit curious about this woman known as the "Hugging Saint."

I left early in the morning and began my drive north up to Santa Fe to find the site of the event. I later found out that the woman known as the "Hugging Saint" goes by the name "Amma" and teaches that her religion is Love.

I arrived at the venue and to my surprise found a large tent set up with hundreds of cars in the parking lot. I don't know why I had assumed this was to be a much smaller gathering. I decided to walk into the tent and find out what was going on inside.

As I entered the back of the huge circus sized white tent, I observed hundreds of people all dressed in white. They were seated in rows of white chairs and there was some East Indian music playing in the background. I had never seen anything like this before. There was an excitement in the air as well as a sacred reverence.

At the front was a beautiful altar and a woman sitting on the stage dressed in white. She had a beautiful, loving presence, which emanated from her being. This had to be "Amma," also known as the "Hugging Saint." People from the audience formed a long line up the center aisle for an opportunity to experience her loving embrace.

I continued to observe this process; as an individual approached her they would first bow in respect and she would give them a blessing. She would then totally embrace them like a mother would hug and hold her child. I noticed after people left the stage they had a peaceful, blissful smile on their face as though they had just been hugged and in the presence of God.

As I said, I had never seen anything like this before and really enjoyed feeling the peace and love in that place. On a more practical note, I knew I would be in line for hours before my opportunity to get on the stage with her. I decided to leave, grateful for this experience. I wanted to reach Durango before nightfall, and drove off feeling a little remorse I was not able to experience the loving hug from this amazing woman.

The Fire-Walking Foot Doctor

Chapter Three

When the Student Is Ready the Teacher Will Appear

I left the "Hugging Saint" event still feeling the peace and love of that space and I eagerly headed north toward Durango, Colorado wondering what I might experience next.

I arrived in town before nightfall and immediately noticed the beauty and serenity of the surrounding mountains. I met up with Pam and it was great to reconnect with her once again.

I told Pam I was going through a detox in my body from the Candida infection in my gut, and she immediately recommended I visit the Mineral Hot Springs bath just north of town.

In the meantime, she had scheduled a reading for me with her friend Anna in two days. Pam said she would help me come up with a list of questions that I might want to ask. She explained that Anna worked with several Ascended Master Teachers such as Archangel Michael, St. Germain, Jesus and Mother Mary. She explained Ascended Masters were great Beings of Light who had once resided in physical bodies like ours. Lifetime after lifetime they accomplished much to help raise humanity, and in the process became so spiritually evolved that they were able to ascend and now reside permanently in the higher spiritual realms. I didn't understand her explanation at the time and didn't give it much thought.

I had never had a psychic reading before and did not know what to expect, but was looking forward to it nonetheless. I did plan my trip to visit the Mineral Hot Springs however.

I awoke early the next day and headed north about 15 miles until I arrived at the Hot Springs. Mineral Hot Springs, as the name implies, have a heavy concentration of minerals, which help draw any toxins out of your body (just what I needed at that time). I also signed up for a deep tissue massage, which was available on site.

As I jumped into the hot water I instantly felt relaxed and was glad I made the trip. After about 30 minutes I was completely stress free and my body really felt much lighter. I then had the deep tissue massage, which totally spaced me out. I now felt totally cleansed and refreshed from the inside out. If you have never experienced hot mineral springs, I highly recommend it.

As I was driving back to Durango, I thought about my reading tomorrow and was looking forward to another new experience. It seems ever since I drove out of Florida to head west that new experiences were becoming commonplace for me. I was excited, as my spiritual journey was well underway.

When I arrived in Durango, I asked Pam to call her friend Anna and invite her to have dinner with us. I figured it would be nice to meet her before the reading, and yes, I was somewhat curious because I never met anyone who did this type of spiritual work before.

We all met at a restaurant later that night and I remember meeting Anna for the first time, like it was yesterday. She was a very nice lady with a southern drawl. I remember looking into her eyes and noticing how clear they were: they seemed to radiate a deep peace from within. (It is said that the eyes are a window into our Souls.) She began to explain to me that she had been given the gift to communicate with higher spiritual beings since she was a child. She grew up in Arkansas and then on a farm in rural Oklahoma (part of the Bible Belt). She had had to keep her ability secret for the most part because of the deeply religious nature of the people in her community. People in that belief system think it is blasphemy if you can communicate with the higher spiritual realms. This is what they were taught and what they believe.

Anna then went on to explain that during a reading one of her spiritual teachers will literally overshadow her and provide her with the answers to the questions. So far so good, I thought. I couldn't wait for tomorrow.

As our dinner continued, she described some of the teachers she works with. Among them were Archangel Michael, St. Germain, Jesus, Mother Mary, Lord Matreya, and Commander Ashtar. I was not familiar with most of these names primarily because I was raised in the Jewish tradition, and also because I was not even aware Ascended Masters existed.

I had never met anyone like Anna before and started asking her many questions. I remember asking her why she wasn't working before thousands of people in large stadiums like the Reverend Billy Graham used to. I mean with her ability to work and communicate directly with Jesus, she could help to inspire many. Her response was that is not my job right now. You know me by now, I then followed up with "well then, what is your job?" She smiled at me and said in the future she will be starting a "City of Light," a place that would produce healing of mind, body and soul using advanced technology not seen on this planet for eons of time.

I remember as she continued to explain and answer my many questions, I did not feel any resistance or disbelief on my part at all. The concept of future "Cities of Light" sure sounded encouraging, especially with all the chaos and human suffering occurring on our planet at this time. She also told me she taught a meditation class which I was more than welcome to attend if I was still in town.

After dinner I went back to Pam's house, my head still spinning from all the information I had received from Anna. She shared much with me over dinner and was so convincing and sincere that I could not help but believe what she was sharing. Pam then sat down with me and helped me come up with a list of questions to ask at my reading tomorrow.

I woke up the next day and couldn't wait to meet Anna for my reading. She did her work in a small church on the other side of town run by some of her friends. It wasn't a typical church, it was a space many spiritual people would utilize for different events. As I entered the small building, she was already there, patiently waiting for me. I first noticed there was no large cross or altar in the room like all the other churches I had been in.

I took my seat opposite her, and she began by saying that Archangel Michael was already present and would do the work with her today. She then closed her eyes and instructed me to begin asking my questions. As I continued to go down my list of questions I was amazed at the personal information this Archangel Michael apparently knew about me. I enjoyed being in his energy and after a while I no longer had to ask the questions as he was able to look at my list and start answering them without me having to verbalize them. I thought, how cool and amazing is this? I did receive a lot of personal information in this reading (which I have chosen not to include here). I finally asked him about the Being of Light who mysteriously appeared to me years ago on my back deck in Ohio. Remember, he was wearing a white robe, had long white hair and a beard. Archangel Michael started to laugh and told me that the Being was one of my Spirit Guides and his name is Matthew. He was one of the Apostles at the time of Jesus and he serves as a kind of guardian angel for you. You and he have worked together in many lifetimes and he helps you now more than you are even aware of. Good to know I have friends in high places! Archangel Michael continued and said that he had appeared for me to offer guidance and help, but I was not ready at that point in my life to accept it. I chose to learn some painful life experiences instead. He continued to explain that all human beings have Free Will, and even though our guides and spiritual teachers carry infinite power which we are not able to truly comprehend, they always have to honor and respect that.

As the session was coming to an end, I asked him if I would ever practice podiatric medicine and surgery again. He responded by saying in the future you will have the healing ability to heal the whole body, not just feet. I was very intrigued by his answer and wondered how on earth would I accomplish this. It was as if he read my mind once again. He told me because of the higher spiritual healing work I had done in past lives, I was chosen and yes volunteered to once again step forward and help heal humanity in any way I could. The time of the reading was now ending, I had so many new questions after his last answer. I thanked him for his help and guidance, and then Anna gently opened her eyes and he was gone.

My head was still spinning about what he just told me. He mentioned past lives (I had never really thought about it), he mentioned I was chosen and volunteered to once again step forward and help heal humanity (not even sure what to think of this information yet). All this just seemed to further validate my decision to shed my past and look forward to a new life, wherever and whatever that might be.

Anna had by now opened her eyes. I looked at her and

was truly amazed at this experience which had lasted about an hour. I first thanked her for helping me in this process. I then asked her what it was like when her guides and teachers overshadow her and speak through her. She just smiled and said I have been doing this for so long I am used to their vibrations and energy and just let them take over. She did admit the process does leave her a little spaced out but that she was used to it.

I thanked her again for this incredible experience and she was very gracious and humble. She explained her teachers deserve all the credit and that they just use her physical form to communicate their information. Before I left, she invited me to attend one of her meditation classes which would take place in a couple of days. I gladly accepted and told her I would see her then.

As I drove back to Pam's house after the reading, my mind was racing. The night before I learned about the future "Cities of Light" and the existence of Ascended Masters. Today I had a reading with a Spiritual Being who was not in a physical body but yet knew everything about me; past, present and future. I felt extremely excited and energized by all of this even if I did not quite understand it. I could not forget the last thing Archangel Michael shared with me. He said I would be doing important healing work in the future to help humanity, work that he said I have done in past lives. Again, I had no time to process any of this, but enjoyed the feeling it gave me anyway. It all sounded so positive and exciting. My experiences so far continued to validate my decision to leave Florida.

I had to learn more about everything! Every new experience so far had raised a million new questions for me. I felt that Anna somehow would play a key role in helping me understand more. Pam and I stayed up late that night as I shared much of the information from my reading. I thanked her again for inviting me to Durango and introducing me to Anna. She smiled and said "I told you she was connected." I now understand what she meant. She was connected to advanced spiritual beings who reside in much higher dimensions of reality than do currently exist here on Earth.

I couldn't wait to attend Anna's meditation class. The next few days seemed to fly by as I was trying to process all this new information I was receiving.

The Fire-Walking Foot Doctor

Chapter Four

My First Meditation Class Experience

It was now two days after my reading and tonight was Anna's meditation class. I could not wait to experience a meditation class, and with Anna's teachers who knew what to expect?

As I entered the church to attend the class, I saw Anna sitting on the far side of the room with chairs placed around her to form a circle. She smiled at me and Pam and motioned for me to take the seat immediately to her left. As I took my seat she introduced me to the rest of the group, and I found everyone to be very welcoming and friendly.

As the class began, Anna once again formally introduced me to the group as a friend of Pam's who was visiting from Florida. She then went into a short lesson about higher spiritual truth, and then it was time for us to meditate.

She began by having the group close their eyes, and she then guided us into doing some deep breathing as a way for us to become totally relaxed and be able to raise our consciousness at the same time. Her voice was very soothing and this made it easier to just breathe and let go as she continued to coach us into going higher and higher. This process continued and I became so relaxed I felt myself once again (as in my Pancha-Karma experience) literally leaving my body out through the top of my head. Wow, I thought, I no longer felt the heavy weight of my physical body, I just felt light, free and totally at peace. I could barely hear her voice by this time as she guided and directed the group up into the God's Magnificent Garden. She then released us there until it was time for her to call us back.

As soon as she became silent, I looked around and found myself on some kind of large vessel which reminded me of something I had seen in a "Star Trek" movie. This large ship (at least this is what I am calling it) had many beings on board who resembled humans so I immediately felt at ease. I was approached by a young man who said he would be acting as my guide. He was very warm in his welcome and very professional as he showed me various areas of the ship. It was far too large to see it all at one time but I found it fascinating nonetheless.

As we continued touring this amazing vessel, he told me because of my medical background (now, wait a minute! I never mentioned that to him, but with all the strange events I recently had experienced I did not feel the need to question him), he was going to show me an area that would greatly interest me. We then entered an area of the ship that I could best describe as the medical clinic. I met the doctor in charge and he briefly showed me some of his very advanced (at least by Earth standards) healing equipment, which he said, in time, would be made available to Earth once again. (Not sure what he meant by saying once again, but I did not dare ask him at this time.) He invited me to return for a visit whenever I wished so I could learn more.

The next thing I heard was Anna's gentle soothing voice guiding us to return to the church and the energy of the room. When we were ready, she asked us to slowly open our eyes.

I want to tell you that when you experience these out-of-body experiences (I'd had two up to this point), they feel every bit as real as anything else you experience in your life.

As I slowly opened my eyes and, reluctantly returned

to the church, my eyes must have had a glaze over them. Anna looked at me and asked if I was okay and I gently responded I think so. She then went around the room asking if anyone wanted to share their meditation experience. She eventually got to me and asked if there was anything I wanted to share with the group. I began to describe my "spaceship" experience and her face seemed to light up with genuine excitement. She seemed very pleased for me and encouraged me to meditate as often as possible.

After the class was over I seemed to now have a million more questions to ask (spaceships, really!?). So Pam and I made plans to see Anna the next day.

When I got back to Pam's house, once again I felt an inner peace and was totally open and accepting of my meditation experience. I had so many questions, but was so tired and decided to sleep on it until tomorrow.

The next day I asked Pam what was there to do around Durango for fun? She replied, why don't we go rafting today, the Animas River runs gently through the center of town and would be fun. I agreed, we then called Anna, and to Pam's surprise she agreed to join us.

After a couple of very relaxing hours on the river, we went for dinner and I now had my chance to ask Anna more questions.

I began right away wanting to know more about spaceships. I never thought about their existence before my experience the previous night, but at the same time never doubted the possibility either. Anna explained that there is a large fleet of spaceships under the command of a being known as Commander Ashtar. She went on to explain that he works closely with Master Jesus and that his fleet of ships patrol the earth and keep it safe within it's orbital pathway. Again, as in other conversations I had had with Anna, I never felt any resistance or disbelief whatsoever. She continued on to say that not all space visitors to earth were of the 'Light' (meaning spiritually evolved). These would explain the ships involved in cattle mutilation and other events commonly seen in the western United States.

I know what you, the reader, must be thinking at this point. Spaceships, really? Extra-terrestrials, really? A commander of a fleet of ships that works with Jesus and God to help protect planet earth, really? All I can say is please keep an open mind because the story gets even more interesting.

The more Anna spoke, the more inquisitive I got. I asked her, "You mean to tell me that Ashtar works with Jesus as part of a Spiritual Hierarchy that works behind the scenes to help protect and elevate humanity?" She smiled and replied, "absolutely!"

Now up to this point in my life (hint, hint) I had never seen a UFO. I had always assumed that there had to be other forms of life in the billions and billions of stars that exist. What I never would have assumed in my wildest imagination would be that some UFOs are connected to God, more specifically to Jesus (if in fact this is true?). This was such a foreign concept to me, but I was open to any and all possibilities at this time.

As our dinner continued, I asked Anna about my meditation experience and the ship I went to visit. She said I was taken aboard what is referred to as a mothership. These are extremely large and can be as big as a city. She said I was taken aboard to meet the doctor, someone I had worked with in a past life and who I would be given an opportunity to work with again in this lifetime if I choose. (Say what?)

If you remember the last thing Archangel Michael told me

in my reading, he said in the future I will learn how to heal the whole human body. Maybe this doctor would teach me how to do it. What! Stop! This is crazy! Have I lost my mind? I report, you decide!!

So let me get this straight. I'm going to have the opportunity to work with Advanced Spiritual Beings, with advanced technology to help heal humanity. Really? Why me? I was starting to wonder what they put in the drinking water here in Durango! Was I imagining all this, or was it all part of a greater plan? I figured time would tell, as it always does.

As our dinner was winding down, Anna said the future "Cities of Light" would have advanced healing and energy technologies handed down from our spiritually advanced space brothers and sisters

I can tell you one thing, this was a dinner conversation I would surely never forget. She recommended I read a book called *The Ashtar Command* which would explain more in detail about much of our conversation.

My time in Durango was coming to an end, as I had plans to go camping with friends up near the Denver, Colorado area. Pam informed me she was facilitating a fire walking ceremony in the second week of July and would I return to assist her? Since everything I had seen and experienced here was largely due to her inviting me for a visit, I immediately said yes and wanted to be of service in any way I could. Also, this place called Durango had so far turned out to be better than Disneyland!

While driving north to Denver for my 4th of July camping weekend, I had a lot of time to think about everything I had experienced during the week. It started with a soothing hot mineral springs bath and massage. Then I had my reading, my meditation class experience, and my dinner with Anna and all she shared about Commander Ashtar and the spaceships. To say my head was spinning would certainly be an understatement. With all this new information I felt a deep sense of amazement, curiosity and even bewilderment. What if everything I was told and shown turned out to be right and correct? I also had a strong sense of excitement about being exposed to future possibilities.

It was good to reconnect with my friends in Denver and I enjoyed the peace of sleeping out in the mountains. I did not share any of my Durango experiences with them because I was still trying to process them myself. After my weekend with them, I felt refreshed and reinvigorated as I said my goodbyes and headed back south toward Durango. On the drive, I felt a sense of excitement not knowing what I would experience or learn next, but I was totally open for anything.

Upon my return to Durango, I reconnected with Pam and Anna the day of the fire walk. Pam asked me if I would tend to the fire and evenly rake the coals in preparation for the people to walk, while she did her facilitating inside the house with all the participants. I said absolutely, and looked forward once again to participate in such a high-energy event.

Night time came early and I drove out to the site of the event to help light the fire. I would remain outside and monitor the fire while the others were inside preparing mentally and emotionally for the event. I enjoyed this time by myself, with the cool evening air and the sky which looked like it had a million shining stars.

At last the group was outside, gathered around the runway of hot coals I had prepared for them. You could feel the excitement, as well as anxiety from the group. Pam gave a few more verbal instructions and then they lined up to begin.

Pam walked across first, and everyone seemed to breathe a

sigh of relief and then began walking themselves. The pure joy and exhilaration one feels when doing this is hard to describe.

Anna then took her place in line and walked across with no issues. After everyone in the group had walked at least once I got in line and walked across the hot coals with a confident big grin on my face. I then asked Anna if she wanted to walk across with me. She said yes and we walked hand in hand to the other side. I really have fun at these events because of the transformation you see in people.

As it so happens I had registered to take a course up in northern California to become a "Certified Fire Walking Instructor" and would leave Durango to drive up there in another day or so.

My time in Durango was now up and I would head all the way up to northern California. I spent my remaining time in Durango with both Pam and Anna, and thanked them for everything. I enjoyed my connection with Anna and promised I would keep in touch with her.

My plans for the rest of my time out west were to attend the five-day certified fire walking course in northern California, return to Albuquerque to spend a few more days with my friends, and then make the long drive back to southern Florida. I intended to begin my backpacking around the world adventure in mid-September 1992.

As I left Durango heading towards northern California, I felt an inner peace which made me incredibly happy. I had no way of knowing just how magical my time in Durango would turn out to be. I was simply grateful for how much fun I was having and enjoyed being in the moment. The future and whatever it might hold would have to wait. Doesn't it always?

The Fire-Walking Foot Doctor

Chapter Five

Becoming A Certified Firewalking Instructor (Why Not?)

The drive to California from Colorado was long, and I was excited for my next adventure. The whole idea to become a certified firewalker instructor appealed to me. With my background as a foot surgeon I would have instant credibility with people (so I thought) should I decide to start facilitating these types of events in the future. At least with a certificate in hand, I believed it would show others that I did my due diligence in studying the proper way to build the fire, the best wood to use, how to prepare people so they can walk safely, and all the other things that went into hosting these events.

Being a doctor, I understood the importance of credentials in today's world. Not knowing if I would ever use this knowledge and experience, I decided to sign up and go for it anyway. I know what you're probably thinking; a school to learn how to be a firewalking instructor, what was I thinking? It was not like this course was mainstream and offered everywhere, so I went where many people go to participate in fringe events, Good Old California!!

I finally arrived at the venue, a beautiful place with tall amazing trees, and rustic cabins spread throughout the property, with a beautiful lake just a short drive away. The catering for this event was all vegetarian and done by the same people who worked with the band "The Grateful Dead" when they were on tour. (Remember, this was mid-July 1992.) Not sure why I am sharing this, but the food was incredible. I did not make the decision to become a vegetarian until some 15 years later. I am sure the quality of this food planted a positive seed in my subconscious to at least consider it.

The total group of people here numbered about twenty-five, and I met individuals from all over the United States. I was the only foot surgeon in the group (no surprise there!!). People seemed impressed and highly amused that someone with my medical background would be interested in doing this firewalking stuff.

The next day our training began with classes throughout the morning and afternoon. We were told we would participate in a fire walk every evening, each one with a different theme or twist to it. I was pleasantly surprised at the structure and detail of the information given. These instructors were very serious about their craft and I enjoyed learning from them.

As the week progressed, I was having a lot of fun. The nightly fire walks were always exhilarating and the energy of this group was full of love and support. I don't know if I had ever been around such positive people, it sure did make for a great time.

The theme for tonight's fire walk was described as a "Buddhist" fire walk, whereby the intent was for at least one person in the group to walk 108 times consecutively across the hot coals. (The significance of the number 108 is prevalent in many traditions. A common meaning is that 108 represents "spiritual completion,") Now who in their right mind would agree to do this?

As the sun set we all completed dinner and gathered around the hot coals once again. There seemed to be a little anxiety within the group tonight due to the nature of this particular fire walk. The instructors once again explained that the intent of tonight's fire walk was for someone to cross 108 times. They also said as this event began it would become very evident which persons or persons would be up for the challenge. I didn't have an opinion or feeling either way as this event was about to start, I was able to focus and stay in the here and now.

We all lined up just like the previous nights and began walking the hot coals. The only difference tonight was that we would circle around and get back in line and repeat the process. One of the instructor's jobs was to be on the sideline and count the number of trips across the coals we had done. When you walk across such hot coals you need to be focused 100% on what you are doing, so counting our own trips across was totally out of the question.

As the fire walk progressed some of the other walkers started dropping out of line. I became aware of this only by the fact that the wait time between walks seemed less. I was incredibly focused during this event. One of my friends who was facilitating this event was banging on a small circular Native American drum and the cadence of that drum seemed to carry me across the coals with little effort on my part. As the number of people walking continued to diminish at a much more rapid rate, I began to pick up my speed and intensity of which I was walking. There were far less people in line now and literally no waiting at all.

I seemed to be getting stronger and more intense as I continued walking at a much faster pace. I asked my friend if I could take her drum and beat on it as I continued to walk. She agreed and now with drum in hand I began beating on it as I continued across the coals. The sound and vibration of that little drum seemed to be raising my consciousness so high that I could barely feel my feet.

I must have been in some sort of trance (an altered state

of consciousness) and noticed that there were only two people still walking, me and another guy I had met from California. During this trance-like state I felt totally at peace, totally focused on walking across the hot coals and could no longer hear any outside sounds or voices other than the beating of my drum. I had never experienced anything like this before in my life and was enjoying it. After a period of time I suddenly heard someone yell out you are now at number one hundred for your trips across the coals.

At first I could not believe that was true. I felt like I had only been walking for a few minutes. I learned whether you are in a deep meditation or any other type of altered state of consciousness, one's sense of time becomes totally distorted and frankly irrelevant.

The group became louder now as they were really cheering and encouraging me and my new friend to finish the fire walk. I was filled with adrenaline and soon thereafter the sense of pride as we both finally crossed the hot coals for the 108 times that evening. Part of me was feeling numb and disbelief, the other part feeling a real sense of accomplishment. Everyone was hugging us and clapping, it was a real celebration of the human spirit.

Even today when I think back on that special night, I don't really understand how that was physically possible. Believe it or not, I did not burn my feet once that night! I will admit the next day the soles of my feet were a little tender, but absolutely no burn or blisters. Incredible, right?

The following day my friend and I (who had also walked the 108 times) took a short drive to a nearby lake and enjoyed putting our feet into the ice cold water. It was very soothing to say the least. That fire walk experience is something I will never forget, and I still enjoy the looks on the people's faces when I share my story with them.

As this workshop was winding down, one night they brought in a professional photographer to shoot pictures of us walking across the hot coals. To my surprise, someone had a stethoscope and a sport coat in their car and I decided to have my picture taken wearing both (refer to the front cover). I thought if I ever went back into medical practice it would make a great conversation piece hanging on the wall in my waiting room.

The week turned out to be a lot of fun, with more spiritual experiences, new friends and contacts. Upon finishing the course we were indeed presented with a certificate, and I felt a real sense of accomplishment and pride. At this time I had no way of knowing if I would ever facilitate any fire walking events, but at least I now felt confident enough if I should ever choose to do so. As I left California I was once again filled with a sense of awe, as my time out west had truly been unbelievable on so many levels.

The Fire-Walking Foot Doctor

Chapter Six

Commander Ashtar (Fact or Fiction?)

Upon my return to New Mexico, I needed to rest for I had been going nonstop for about three weeks. I shared my many experiences with my friends and they were excited for me. They could definitely see and feel the difference in me since I had first arrived more than a month ago. How could I not be different after all I had seen and experienced.

One day I decided to call Anna in Durango, just to check in and share my fire walking school experience with her. She seemed excited to hear from me and quickly told me about an upcoming trip she was taking to northern New Mexico to visit her friend Myra. She further explained that a group of advanced spiritual people would be in attendance as well. She told me that she got permission from her Spiritual Guides to invite me to join the group. Now here was the kicker!! She said "Commander Ashtar" promised to make an appearance in one of his spaceships!!

That's right, you heard me correctly. I was being given the opportunity to see a UFO at a planned date, time, and location, not a random sighting. What would you have done? I quickly agreed to go. As strange as my time out west had been I was totally open to this next adventure.

If you remember, on my first visit to Durango, Anna explained to me that "Ashtar" was a fleet commander for a vast amount of ships currently patrolling and protecting planet Earth. On top of this, she stated that he worked closely with Jesus and other members of the spiritual hierarchy representing God. (I know, I hear you. Crazy right?)

I soon found myself driving once again up to northern New Mexico to meet another group of people, not sure what to expect. I arrived at Myra's house early on a Friday afternoon and entered into a room full of people waiting to be seen by her. Anna immediately greeted me, introduced me to Myra and further explained she was a healer and the people waiting were her clients.

Myra was a short woman with silver hair and piercing brilliant blue eyes. She invited me to observe her at work and I found this very interesting. She would have a person lie down on the small exam table and then use her own hand (palm facing downward) to scan from the top of the head to the bottom of their feet. Her hand would stop when she felt and sensed any type of abnormality. She would then explain what she found to the person and what they needed to do to be healed. I had never seen anything like this before and couldn't take my eyes off what she was doing. It was as if she was using her hand like an x-ray machine and revealing what she psychically saw and felt. She quickly went through all the people in her waiting room and Anna told me to get on the table and let Myra work on me. I jumped at this opportunity and was totally open to what she might find and do. (Now if you remember, I was diagnosed about a month earlier with a Candida yeast infection in my stomach and was still taking medication and following a strict diet).

As I lay on my back on the exam table, Myra opened her hand palm down and a few inches above my forehead and slowly started scanning my body. When she reached my stomach area she abruptly stopped her hand and said "you are currently experiencing an imbalance in your stomach and intestines, but do not worry you will soon be completely healed." To say I was stunned at her accurate diagnosis would be an understatement! How did she know this? As I got up off the table both Anna and Myra were laughing at the stunned look on my face. I joined in and started laughing myself.

I asked Myra how she was able to do the work she does. I had never seen anything like this before and I now experienced it firsthand. She explained to me that since she was a child she had the ability to see and feel things that other people do not. When she is working on people, she either sees something in their body or feels something abnormal and then intuitively knows how to correct it. What an amazing gift she has, and good for her for sharing this ability to help others. My long strange journey continues!

Later that evening the group had all assembled and Anna began channeling (communicating) directly with Ashtar. I had seen her do this before during my reading and still found it fascinating. Ashtar said he would show up the following evening immediately after sundown. Everyone in the group was very excited to hear this. The back of Myra's house faced some mountains and there was about a half mile of land separating her backyard from these mountains. I thought this would be as good a place as any for a flyby.

The next day couldn't come fast enough for me. I was so excited to see what was going to take place that I had a hard time sleeping the night before. The group met again during the day and once again Ashtar confirmed he would be coming around sundown. He instructed us all to be seated outside in the backyard, facing the mountains just before the sun disappeared behind the mountains. There were a total of eight people in the group and the excitement continued to build all day. We broke for an early dinner and all met back at Myra's in plenty of time to observe the sunset.

As the sun began to go down, we all went outside and lined up our chairs facing these magic mountains. We all sat waiting for something to occur, and then Ashtar once again communicated directly with Anna, and said there might be a possibility we could be physically taken aboard one of the ships. Now our excitement level was totally off the charts. I thought to myself, could this really be happening?

As dusk slowly turned into darkness, I could not help but feel the majesty of the beautiful mountains. During this time Anna was in constant contact with Ashtar and he confirmed he was nearby. My heart began to beat wildly with excitement and in a few moments, to my surprise, we observed three lights in the sky moving toward us. Was this really happening?

Soon they appeared closer and there were three ships with their lights on so we could see them. The lights appeared to radiate a green hue as they began to put on a show for us. These small ships were totally quiet as they flew back and forth across the night sky.

They began doing zigzag maneuvers which appeared to totally defy the law of gravity as I understood it. Their movements reminded me of water bugs who on the surface of water can stop and start and move in random angles at will. Now here were flying machines of some type doing the same thing in the air, able to defy gravity as if it didn't exist. Watching this aerial show seemed quite surreal, as had many of my experiences on this trip out west.

In the past I had heard of and read different accounts of people having had random sightings of so-called UFOs, but I was not aware of any which were scheduled in advance like this one. The ships continued to fly and maneuver around to our joy and amazement, and then in an instant suddenly departed.

Ashtar once again communicated through Anna, and conveyed his apologies for having to leave so abruptly, explaining they had an emergency situation that needed their help and attention at this time.

The group including myself were all still extremely jazzed up from this experience and yes, a little disappointed we were not able to physically go aboard one of these ships.

All I could think or say was WOW! How does one process this type of eyewitness experience? For me I chose to do it very carefully and confidentially, at least at first. It has now been about 25 years since this event took place and with numerous other documented eyewitness accounts of UFO sightings, I feel much more comfortable sharing this information at this time.

After this night's eyewitness, and yes, mind-blowing experience, how could I not totally believe Anna's story about future "Cities of Light"? How could I not believe that Commander Ashtar was real? How could I not now believe that there is a lot more to life on this planet than the majority of people are aware of? And how could I not believe that this and all my other experiences this summer would not change me forever? The answer is simple, I couldn't.

After the ships left, we all went back inside the house still buzzing about what we saw. I immediately thanked Anna and her teachers for inviting me to come here and allow me to learn the truth about the existence of UFOs and Commander Ashtar. She just smiled back at me and was happy I was having so much fun taking all this in. After a few minutes the group calmed down and Anna once again shared with the group Ashtar's apology for his abrupt departure.

I looked across the room and noticed Myra had her eyes closed and appeared to be receiving some information of her own. She then opened her eyes and gazed across the room at Anna and asked if she had just received the same message. Anna looked a little befuddled and did not immediately give a verbal response. Myra said she just received a message that Anna and I were "Twin Rays" and wanted to know if Anna got the same message. This time Anna responded with a yes, but seemed stunned in disbelief for a moment. Everyone in the group seemed extremely happy about this except me, because I didn't understand what a "Twin Ray" was.

Myra went on to explain that when a soul is created out of God's Fire Light, it is then split in two and referred to as "Twin Rays" or "Twin Flames." Basically it means that these two individuals share the same soul light (kind of like different sides of the same coin). It is very rare for Twin Rays to be in a physical body at the same time, let alone meet each other when they are. She went on to explain that usually one Twin Ray stays back in spirit to help support the other one from the higher realms of existence. (If you are confused at all by this, so was I.)

She continued, when "Twin Rays" meet each other in a physical embodiment it is because they have important work to do. When Twin Rays combine their efforts and energy to be of service, the sum of their power is far far greater than if they acted alone. With all the congratulatory remarks from the group, this new information seemed to be a big deal. I was not yet able to fully comprehend it all at this time. Anna then confirmed with Jesus and St. Germain that we were indeed Twin Rays.

Can I say wow again? This was heavy stuff and at the same time I still did not totally understand what it all meant. After this revelation it did seem to cement the bond we had already formed.

It appears that the reason I really chose to go to Taos, New Mexico years previously (to attend a self-empowerment seminar) was to meet Pam, who would in turn serve as the bridge to connect me to Anna. If this was in fact true, it appears our Spirit Guides (which we all have regardless of our individual belief systems) are able to give us subtle, or maybe not so subtle, pushes or shoves in the right direction to help us on our spiritual journey on earth. Whether you are conscious of it or not, all human beings are on a spiritual journey when they inhabit the physical form. The lesson here is if you feel a strong inclination to go do something, trust your gut and go for it. I was taught there is no such thing as a coincidence, so always pay attention when people, places or things are placed in your path.

Now what does the significance of Anna and I being Twin Rays have on my future? So now what am I supposed to do? I had a trip of a lifetime already planned to start in a few short weeks and was looking forward to it.

Anna got clarity from her guides and they said it was up to me if I still wanted to travel around the world. They continued on to say that because of Free Will I would also be given the choice of whether I wanted to work with Anna at the "City of Light" in the future.

What would you have done? I had been out west for awhile now and experienced things, saw things, learned things and felt things that insured I would not and could not be the same person ever again. I desperately wanted a new life and it appeared one was being offered to me. Everything still felt a little overwhelming, yet most of it felt right and correct to me. I decided to still take my backpacking trip around the world and would decide about this "Future City of Light" thing upon my return. I did stay in contact with Anna much of the time from places around the world. The connection we had, transcended any normal third dimensional relationship, but for now I would put that on the back burner.

The next day I returned to Albuquerque to share more of my experience with my friends. I thanked them again for allowing me to use their home as an anchor while visiting the southwest. In a few days I said goodbye and headed back to Florida where I would begin my around the world adventure in September of 1992.

All I can say is, TRUTH IS STRANGER THAN FICTION SOMETIMES. It definitely was for me in the summer of 1992!!!

Chapter Seven

Backpacking 101

I arrived in south Florida thoroughly exhausted from the long drive from New Mexico. It was now August of 1992 and I would start packing and making arrangements for my upcoming trip abroad, which would start in about a month.

During my long drive east, I had plenty of time to think about and process much of what I learned, saw and experienced over the summer. My time with Anna in Durango had forever changed me on more levels than I could possibly understand: From my reading with her, my eyewitness experience seeing Ashtar's ships, learning about future "Cities of Light" and my possible role in those, and then finally to learn she was my "Twin Ray." My trip to Durango had certainly been no coincidence and would prove to have an influence on everything in my life from that moment forward. Having said that, for now I just wanted to go play and have some fun.

Planning an around-the-world trip can be a complicated and tiring process, but instead I chose to carry a backpack, travel light and be spontaneous. I met a couple who had done this kind of trip a few years earlier and they shared their itinerary with me, which I used as a rough guide.

I would travel for about six months touring Nepal, Thailand, Malaysia, Singapore, Indonesia, Australia, New Zealand and Fiji before returning home to rest and regroup.

The second leg of my trip would include parts of Europe (England and Greece), then down to Africa visiting Kenya, Tanzania, Zimbabwe, and South Africa. Then on to Israel,

Egypt, and finally to Peru to visit Machu Picchu.

There is a company called Lonely Planet which publishes very detailed travel guides for just about every country you can imagine. I relied on these heavily, and they never let me down.

With all my spiritual experiences from the summer, I hoped my travels would continue to provide me with more knowledge, experiences, and insight.

I am going to gloss over and skip much of the details of my travels because they only played a small part in my total spiritual awakening. I will, however, include things I found spiritually uplifting, unique or humorous.

September 1992 came quickly and I found myself on a plane heading to Singapore, with backpack in hand and gold credit card in pocket. I was ready for the adventure of a lifetime and had no preconceived notions about what to expect.

For the first time in my adult life I gave myself permission to just live day by day. I would eat when I was hungry and sleep when I was tired.

I arrived in Singapore for a short layover before heading on to Bali, Indonesia in a couple of days. My guidebook warned me that it was illegal to chew gum in Singapore and that you could be fined for not flushing a toilet. In the back of my mind I was curious about how you could enforce such laws; did they have something called the bathroom police? Singapore had many strict rules, but I have to tell you it was by far the cleanest and safest place I had ever been to.

The following day I was walking down the street still feeling jet-lagged and I saw a sign for reflexology. I knew that reflexology involved different pressure points on the foot, which supposedly were connected to different organs in the body. My whole body was tired so I decided to go in and try this reflexology stuff. I entered the office and noticed three elderly oriental women sitting around having a conversation in Chinese. One looked up at me and in broken English asked if I was interested in receiving a treatment. I said yes and shortly my feet were being soaked in a small tub. Once my feet were cleaned and dried, I sat on a flat table with my legs extending over the edge.

As my session began, the first thing I noticed was the incredibly strong grip and fingers this woman had, and the second thing was that this was not your typical relaxing foot massage. She began methodically pressing in to areas of my feet and toes that literally brought tears to my eyes. As I looked across the room at the other two women, they seemed to be enjoying my reaction to this treatment, which made me even more determined to grin and bear my discomfort. I tell you, this was turning out to be incredibly painful but I remained silent and let her finish.

When she was done she smiled at me and I thanked her and quickly left. When I first stood up I could barely feel the soles of my feet. My whole body felt incredibly relaxed and I remember going back to my hotel room and sleeping for the rest of the day.

My advice on Singapore is this: do not chew gum! Make sure you always flush the toilets! And by all means you have got to try reflexology!

I flew to Bali, Indonesia the next day and quickly felt the change in energy. Bali is famous for its sights, sounds, music and smells. It took me one day to unwind and fit in to the rhythm of this magical place. I bought some clothing that the locals wore and this helped me feel more in touch with my new surroundings. There were beautiful temples everywhere you went with amazing flowers and hypnotic music always heard in the background. I traveled to Ubud, the spiritual center of Bali, up in the mountains. On the drive up there were the most incredible green, lush terraced rice fields literally carved into the mountainsides. (Rice is a mainstay crop in this region and hunger is not an issue.) This place felt very spiritual and peaceful so I decided to stay here for a few weeks and do some exploring.

Hinduism is practiced by the majority of people here and you find symbolic statues in every home and business you enter. The more time you spend here the easier it is to just lose yourself in the energy and culture.

I remember walking through the countryside one day and observing three generations of one family sitting on their front porch all working together in the family business of wood carving. Each family member was assigned a different task, even the small children were involved in painting the carvings. I noticed how in this culture families had deep respect for their elders and how tight-knit these families were. Here I was, halfway around the world, and I realized family is family no matter where you are.

I spent a lot of time in Indonesia visiting its many different islands. Each island was unique and offered much in the way of culture and tradition. The final island I visited was called Irian Jaya and was the easternmost part of Indonesia. I flew into the central part of the island (which was at the time not accessible by road) to visit some primitive tribes who 20 years earlier were still practicing headhunting. Really? Yes, Really!

As I got off the plane I heard someone in English ask me if I needed a guide, and I immediately said yes. Turns out his village had a special hut they rented out to tourists. This was perfect, as I wanted to live in a village and really get to experience first-hand what they were like. The village consisted of about 12 huts and did not have electricity or running water. He showed me to my hut, which I found clean and very accommodating. He then introduced me to the Chief of his village. (I had read to bring cigarettes as a gift and sign of respect, which I did.) The Chief seemed excited about meeting me and even more excited about the two cartons of cigarettes I gave to him.

I asked my guide how cigarettes got introduced to the village and he replied the church missionaries would come and pass them out to entice people to attend Sunday services. I thought to myself, really?

Later that evening all the men gathered around in the Chief's hut and I was invited to join them. Through my interpreter they asked questions about my culture and I was able to ask questions about theirs. They asked how many wives were men allowed to have in my culture and when I said only one they all started laughing uncontrollably. Apparently in their culture you could have as many wives as you could afford. (Livestock, namely pigs, were their currency of choice.) I couldn't believe a lot of what they shared with me that night but I found it all fascinating. I felt like I was in a national geographic documentary or something. Here I was connecting with the members of this primitive tribe and I was having a good time.

The mood in the hut suddenly changed and became quite somber. The Chief, with tears in his eyes, was expressing his concerns over maintaining their traditional ways of life. Apparently the government had plans to build roads into this area, in order to cut down the dense rain forest for profit. He feared when this happened it would disrupt the only way of life his people have known for hundreds of years. I felt compassion for these people, and even though I had just met them, I liked them a lot. I asked one last question and that was about being headhunters. They explained if someone from another village killed one of their tribe members they were compelled to kill and eat the person responsible, in order to free the soul of their lost family member. Wow! Strange indeed! They did reassure me with a smile that they no longer practiced this. (Good to know, as I then excused myself and went to sleep.) For the record, I think I slept with one eye open that night just in case something got lost in translation!

The next day a few men were busy digging a hole in the ground which would later serve as an oven. Sweet potatoes were the main staple of this tribe. They would wrap sweet potatoes in large banana leaves, build a fire to heat rocks, then place the rocks and sweet potatoes in the hole to cook. I imagine this was a cooking technique that they had been using for generations.

As I watched them remove the heated rocks from the fire, I noticed they left all the hot coals sitting there on the ground. I do not know what possessed me next, but I asked my guide if he wanted to walk across those hot coals with me in our bare feet. He looked at me and at first thought I was joking. Once he knew I was serious he said okay. He then spoke in his native language and suddenly the whole tribe emerged from their huts to watch us.

I would have loved to know exactly what he said to them. I can imagine he said something like, hey come out and watch this crazy tourist walk over the hot coals. I am sure no tribe member ever in his wildest imagination ever thought to do this. Why would they? I found this whole thing spontaneous and funny at the same time.

I stood on one side of the coals, took a moment to center myself and focus, and then walked across in my bare feet. My guide soon followed me across the coals and many of the villagers were now smiling and laughing. (I am sure to this day this tribe still talks about the crazy tourist who walked across the hot coals.)

Wait, this story gets even better. After my guide and I walked, to my surprise half the village including young children lined up and also walked across the coals that day. They were really having fun and I loved it! Initially I was stunned at how so many people wanted to participate. My guide explained that because I was a guest in their village, they were doing this out of respect for me. My eyes suddenly teared up, and all I could think to do was start clapping. I then looked them all in their eyes trying to show them my appreciation and respect.

Wow! Another heartfelt connection with these incredible people. Who would have ever thought I would fire walk with a tribe of people who in recent history had been headhunters? I for one never did!

I had spent a lot of time exploring many different Indonesian islands but never connected with a group like I had in Irian Jaya. They touched my heart and I hope and pray they are still there. I was grateful for this opportunity to actually live with them and share some incredible moments as well. To spend time with a group of people so entrenched in a different culture was very enlightening.

As I continued my journey through many different places, the weeks just seemed to fly by. I met many interesting people from all over the world and enjoyed being exposed to many different traditions. I never stopped thinking about Anna and the incredible experiences I had back in Durango. I was not sure if I would ever go back there again, but it was something I still thought about a lot.

After my experience in Irian Jaya I flew back to Jakarta, the capital city of Indonesia. Spending time in a village with no running water or electricity, I immediately checked into a five-star hotel and then took the longest shower of my life. It really is amazing how much we take for granted in life. Many people throughout the world do not even have safe drinking water, electricity or a safe level of hygiene.

I was feeling a little homesick and found a Hard Rock Café just down the street from my hotel. After a couple of beers and two cheeseburgers I felt much better. I even called my brother to let him know I was still alive, as I had not called him in about two months.

My experiences in Indonesia allowed me to go off the beaten track and totally disconnect from my sense of reality. To say I left my comfort zone would be an understatement. I am grateful to the many local people I met, some who even invited me into their homes and daily lives. Regardless of where they live, how they dress, how they talk, what they believe in and even what they eat, the common theme is that ALL HUMAN BEINGS ARE CONNECTED AND ONE!!!

After a couple of days of pure luxury, feeling totally rejuvenated I was off to Thailand.

I arrived in Chang Mai in northern Thailand, and immediately went to a youth hostel and signed up for a five-day trek up in the mountains. This trip would include extensive hiking, riding elephants through the jungle, bamboo rafting through a mountain river and staying with locals in a remote mountain village. I loved doing these off-the-beaten-path adventures because you never knew what to expect.

The majority of the people in this region were devout Buddhists. I had never been exposed to Buddhism and asked someone what it meant to them in their life. The young man explained that he lived his life always trying to be kind to others so as not to create any negative karma for himself. The simplest concept of Karma is what you put out in thought and action will eventually return to you. In Buddhism they strongly believe that negative karma has a direct relationship to the quality of your next life on earth. The idea of reincarnation is deeply woven in their belief system and motivates them to be respectful of all life, something our western culture could certainly learn and benefit from.

The day came to begin the mountain trek and there were ten people in the group and two guides. One of the highlights for me was riding a massive elephant through the thick jungle. I felt like I was in a Tarzan movie and really had fun. After the elephant ride we were then led to a rapidly flowing river to begin our bamboo rafting adventure.

As a side note, if you have never been in a real jungle it is a unique experience. All throughout our journey both of our guides were constantly educating us about the medicinal properties of many plants and trees. I found this extremely interesting and was shown different plants that could stop bleeding, heal wounds and some even had antibiotic properties. Who knew the jungle was a pharmacy? I didn't, and enjoyed learning all I could about Mother Nature.

Wherever I traveled, I was always impressed by how clever and adaptable human beings are to their immediate living conditions and environment. You can imagine how long it must have taken for mankind to learn the different medicinal uses of the plants, trees, and herbs easily found in this jungle region.

It was now time to climb on the bamboo rafts for a short journey down river to a remote village where we would spend the night. These rafts were cleverly constructed and surprisingly well balanced as we navigated the current and small rapids we encountered. I was impressed with the ingenuity of the people who originally came up with the idea and design for this functional way of navigating a river.

We arrived at our destination and it was a small village nestled up in the mountains, yet with river access nearby. We were taken in to a larger two-room hut which was the home of some locals. We all put our gear in one room as the family lived in the other room with their cozy fire keeping that room warm and comfortable.

We met the family and they were very friendly and welcoming to our group even though they spoke no English. I couldn't help but notice that the father of this family suffered from severe arthritis in his hand, and by the way he walked his knees were affected as well. I had an emergency medical kit with me as well as some basic meds. Through our guide I offered to give him a pain pill to help alleviate his pain. He quickly accepted my offer and I gave him a Tylenol #4 tablet with codeine. Within an hour his whole demeanor changed and he started laughing and making jokes in his native language. I was happy he was feeling better and could only wonder how long it had been since he felt any relief from the pain. He later came up to me and hugged me and then insisted I spend the night with his family in their private room with the warm fire. (Kindness does have it's perks!)

I again felt a strong connection with another human being even though we spoke different languages. We left the following morning and I made sure to give him a few more pills. I always help people when I can and sometimes all it takes is kindness and a smile, no words required.

After touring most of Thailand, I was off to Katmandu, Nepal. This city had a spiritual vibe about it like no other. There were numerous temples and holy sites scattered throughout this area, which contributed to the sacred and peaceful feeling here. Katmandu also serves as a jumping off point to go trekking in the Himalayan Mountains and Mt. Everest. This place had a magical energy to it and even thinking about it brings back that feeling of inner peace. After a couple of days of exploring the city and it's sacred temples, it was now time to fly up to the base of the Himalayan Mountains for a few days of trekking.

Getting off the plane you could immediately feel the high altitude and a sense of light-headedness. It was recommended to stay in a local hostel for twenty-four hours, to allow your body time to acclimate to the altitude before embarking on your trek, which I did.

I tell you, walking through these sacred mountains was very exhilarating and challenging. One day on the trail I noticed a small Buddhist temple in the distance. I decided to stop in to take a break and was immediately offered some yak tea by one of the monks. On the other side of the room an elderly monk began chanting in a very rhythmic pattern. I soon closed my eyes and my body began swaying back and forth to his powerful chanting. I don't know how long this went on for, but eventually he stopped his chant and I remember slowly opening my eyes and noticed he was grinning at me, nodding in approval. This experience energized me for the rest of the day.

After a couple more days of hiking, I was finally able to get a glimpse of Mt. Everest in the distance. I felt this was quite an accomplishment, as every day the altitude was increasingly putting more stress on my body. I was grateful for the opportunity to walk these narrow trails, and will never forget how liberating it felt to be in those majestic mountains.

After returning to Katmandu for a couple of days, I was off to Australia and then New Zealand.

The Fire-Walking Foot Doctor

I had been on my trip now for many months and was looking forward to resting in Australia. I had heard it was similar to America in a lot of ways, but with fewer people and much less stress. People in Australia seemed happy and seemed to enjoy their lives as much as they could. One Australian told me that he works to live, and doesn't live to work. This attitude of working to live seemed quite prevalent, and wherever I went I found spirited people having fun.

I entered Australia on the northern coast city of Darwin and then eventually worked my way down the east coast through Brisbane, Bryon Bay, Sydney, and eventually Melbourne. I love Australia, it is a beautiful place not overly populated, and full of positive fun loving people. It was nice for a change to be out of the third world countries I had visited, and being here felt like more of a true vacation. This is definitely a country I would like to return to some day. I enjoyed the cities and the beautiful countryside, as well as the beaches. The people here have a great fun loving demeanor about them which was fun to be around. You should definitely add this country to your bucket list, and if you don't have a bucket list yet, WHAT ARE YOU WAITING FOR?????

It was now time to fly to New Zealand and do more exploring. New Zealand consists of two islands, one north and one south. These islands ended up having some of the most beautiful terrain and landscapes of anywhere in the world. Remember the "Lord of the Rings" movies? They were filmed in New Zealand.

I thought Australians were fun to be around, but I found the people of New Zealand raised the bar by being incredibly adventurous and borderline crazy. After all, New Zealanders invented bungee jumping. So let's get this straight, one day someone was standing on the middle of a bridge thinking that he would like to jump off said bridge with an oversized rubber band tied around his ankles! (I rest my case, your honor!) By the way, I did go visit the bridge where bungee jumping originated and observed many people willing to take the plunge. I was not one of them, as I felt I had played daredevil enough in my life and didn't want to press my luck!

There is one activity I recommend you try and it is called "Blackwater Rafting". You do this on the north island in a city called Waitomo. An underground river is there with rapids which you float down in huge inflatable inner tubes. They provide you with a wetsuit and hardhat similar to what miners wear with a light attached. As you start down the river the light on your hats are turned on so you can see ahead of you. Eventually you are instructed to turn your light off and turn your attention to the ceiling of this underground cave. All of a sudden you see what looks like thousands of bright, sparkling glowworms on the ceiling of this cave. It gives you the sensation of floating in outer space. The glowworms resemble stars in a dark night sky and to see them while floating down this river was flat out awesome!

If you enjoy being adventurous and participating in outdoor activities and challenges, New Zealand is the place for you. Being that both islands are so small, the whole country has a very laid back feel, and it is very easy to navigate on your own. Just remember to bring plenty of sunscreen, as there is a hole in their ozone layer.

I enjoyed my two weeks there but now it was time to head back east towards America. The final stop on this leg of my itinerary was the island nation of Fiji.

Upon landing in the capital of Fiji, I immediately made my way to a small island resort off the mainland called Beach Comber Island. This was an all-inclusive resort and I was interested in resting and relaxing before my long flight back home.

One part of the island resort was for the guests, the other side had a small village which housed all the employees. This was a beautiful lush island and the clear water offered the best snorkeling I had ever experienced. Everyone was very friendly and this was a perfect place to just chill.

One morning at breakfast I heard a loud crash. I looked up and in the distance I saw that one of the employees had severely cut his hand on a pane of glass which had come crashing down on him. I stopped eating and immediately ran to offer my assistance. His right index finger was cut pretty bad and was bleeding profusely. I immediately put pressure on the cut until someone brought an emergency medical kit which had a tourniquet in it which I applied on his finger. Luckily, at the dive center they had some local anesthetic and sutures which I was able to use to sew up his finger. Everyone involved offered their gratitude to me and I humbly accepted their thanks. I was glad to help, because by the time this guy would have gotten to a hospital he probably would have lost his finger due to infection or because of massive blood loss.

Later that night I noticed the house band was short a guitar player. I asked why and they told me he left the island because his wife was having a baby. Having played guitar in a reggae band in south Florida, I volunteered to sit in with them and they happily accepted my offer. I was excited because I love playing guitar with other musicians and it is a great way to connect on a Soul level. We all connected musically and became friends rapidly.

The next day many of the employees were thanking me for helping one of their own when he cut his hand. Even the kitchen staff made sure I had more than enough to eat. All this attention made me a little uncomfortable, but I did appreciate their gratitude. After I finished breakfast, one of the locals came up to me and presented me with a small hand carved wooden boat with the following carved inscription:

Dr. Cohen, R.
Beach Comber Island

I looked around and all the staff was smiling at me as I graciously and somewhat embarrassingly accepted their gift. Wow! This really touched my heart and I still have that boat today some twenty-five years later. The whole village of locals made me feel welcome and even invited me to take part in a traditional Kava Ceremony later that day.

I was invited to enter their village (which was normally off limits to all resort guests) and as I did, everyone was smiling and made me feel very welcomed. A Kava Ceremony is a traditional way of welcoming visitors to one's village and involves the drinking of a ground up root mixed with water called Kava.

They treated me like an honored guest and I soon observed this ceremony had a somewhat serious, almost religious, type of energy about it. Everyone sat on the floor in a large circle and they started to mix the root with water in a large bowl. Once the mixture was finished they would pour it into a cup made from a coconut, and pass it around one person at a time. The Kava, which looked and tasted like muddy water ,produced a numbing effect around my mouth as well as a deep sense of relaxation. After a few more rounds of drinking this Kava the ceremony was now over, and I thanked everyone for allowing me to participate.

It was now time for dinner and then I would sit in again

with the house band. I had no way of knowing the intoxicating effect this Kava would have on me. All I know was, as I played guitar that night my fingers felt like they weighed 100 pounds each and had a mind of their own. Playing was definitely a challenge, but who cares, I was feeling extremely mellow. My musician friends thought it was funny and had no reservations in teasing me about it. We all laughed the whole night and everyone seemed to be happy. My time on the island was fun and very rewarding as I made many new friends. One of the musicians invited me back to his house on the mainland to spend the night and meet his wife and kids. Since it was time for me to leave Beach Comber Island, I gladly accepted his offer. As we left the resort and headed by boat to the mainland I felt a little sad to be leaving.

My last night in Fiji was at my new friend's house with his wife and two kids. They were very nice and welcoming, as were all the people in Fiji who displayed incredible hospitality. When it came time for dinner we all sat on the floor on bamboo mats and my friend motioned me to sit at the head of these mats. He was honoring me as a guest in his home and then placed a large fully cooked fish directly in front of me. He explained their tradition, when a guest was having a meal that the food was offered to them first and that they should eat as much as they wanted. When the guest was finished the family would then share whatever food was left. I thanked him for his hospitality, but insisted we all eat together at the same time, which brought big big smiles to the faces of his children. I was touched by the warmth and generosity of he and his family. What a great way to spend my last night in Fiji!

Well, the first leg of my around-the-world adventure was now complete, and I began my long flight back to Florida. I couldn't believe all I had seen and experienced. What meant even more to me was all the human connections I made along the way. For any of you interested in taking a trip similar to mine, I would highly recommend you visit any third world countries first. The lack of infrastructure can make it more physically and mentally challenging as well as draining.

My advice for traveling abroad is to get out of the big five-star hotels and meet and mingle with the locals, they are the REAL MAGIC regardless of what country you are visiting.

The Fire-Walking Foot Doctor

Chapter Eight

Backpacking 102

Returning home to Florida, I was glad to be back and spent a whole week just catching up on sleep. A trip like mine at times felt like an endurance test, especially my months exploring Indonesia, Thailand and Nepal.

One of the big lessons I learned from being away so long is that in America we may have the highest standard of living, but not necessarily the highest quality of life. What I mean is, compared to the rest of the world our infrastructure, food, water, medicine, technology, hygiene and sanitation services are second to none. However, with our fast paced, fast food, and high stressed way of life (not to mention many of us just live to work), a lot of us don't take enough time out to simply enjoy life.

If you have traveled outside the United States, you observe in many countries businesses close down for a few hours each afternoon so people can enjoy a long relaxing lunch and spend time with their families.

I think people would be happier if they just learned to slow down a little. (You know, smell the roses kind of cliché.) From a spiritual perspective, daily meditation can help people be more relaxed and slow their minds a bit as well.

I had been guilty of working too much myself, with multiple offices in different states at the same time. I can remember it took all my free time and energy, to just physically and mentally survive.

After spending months away from the daily grind of work

and stress, I was able to enjoy and appreciate the simpler, quieter moments of life that pass many of us by when we are too busy. I am definitely not trying to preach here, just hoping that people would learn to slow their lives down and make more quality time for family, friends, hobbies, travel, spiritual practice or anything else that brings joy and happiness to their heart. Life is far too short and valuable not to!!

As I began to think about and plan the next leg of my journey, I was in constant contact with Anna. I told her I was planning to visit Israel and Egypt and she expressed an interest in possibly joining me on this segment. She said she would check with her Spiritual Teachers and get back with me.

In the meantime, my new itinerary would begin in London and then on to Africa. I had always wanted to go on safari and observe animals in their natural habitat. I was definitely NOT interested in shooting anything, unless it was with my camera!! (And yes, I had learned from my days of being Uncle No Film to always check the camera for film before shooting!)

Anna got back to me fairly quickly and said her teachers told her she could go to Israel and Egypt with me. I asked her why she needed their permission and she replied she didn't go anywhere unless they could guarantee her safety. I accepted her explanation without giving it much thought and we then worked out the dates and details of where and when we would meet.

It was now early March of 1993 and I decided to spend the month of April touring throughout Africa. I would then meet up with Anna in London at the beginning of May. From London we would travel together to Israel and then Egypt.

My time back in Florida proved to be somewhat interesting as well. The time spent with friends felt different than before I had made my trip. I felt more disconnected from them and

I could sense they saw me differently as well. How could I not have changed and been a little different after all I had seen and experienced on my trip? (Not to mention all the spiritual awakenings from the previous summer.)

One day I made plans to meet a friend for lunch and she asked if a couple of her friends could join us. I said absolutely and we all met for lunch the next day. I remember sitting at the table listening to their conversations about their day-to-day reality and I could not relate whatsoever. I also shared some of my travel experiences with them and could feel they were not relating to anything I talked abut either.

For the first time I realized what a different time and space I was living in compared to most people. Part of me wondered whether I would ever be able to fit in again. This would have to be a subject for another day, as I was again leaving the country in about two weeks and had a lot to do to prepare for my trip.

Time flew by and I soon found myself back on a plane, this time heading for England, to continue my adventures. I had been to London a few times previously and liked being there, partly because my father's family was from there and I could relate to the people better. I stayed in London a few days so I could adjust to the time change and then I flew off to Harare, Zimbabwe to begin my time in Africa.

Upon arriving in Zimbabwe, I immediately checked into my hotel and searched for a travel agency nearby. I wanted to go see the world-famous Victoria Falls in the northern part of the country as well as whitewater raft down the Zambezi river.

I found a small agency within walking distance of my hotel and struck up a friendly conversation with the owner. I told him I was interested in not only seeing Victoria Falls but that I also wanted to go on safari and see a lot of animals as well. He recommended I go to Tanzania (a country just northeast of Zimbabwe) and guaranteed I would be able to see every kind of animal I wanted. He found a ten-day tour in Tanzania run by a friend of his and said it was to start in a few days. He got me an incredible deal because it was at such a late date and I only had to pay 25% of what all the other people were charged. I promised him I would keep that information to myself and not share it with the rest of the group. This opportunity was too good to pass up and I figured after my safari I would return to Zimbabwe and then go north to explore Victoria Falls.

It was a real blessing to be able to be so spontaneous and take advantage of great opportunities when they were presented. After I booked the tour and my flights, the owner of the travel agency invited me to have lunch with him at his country club.

This was now April of 1993. I soon observed that racial inequality was still quite evident in Africa. The owner of the travel agency was a white male, probably in his mid to late forties and after he had a few drinks he started to display his true racist nature. All the employees at his club were black, wearing white jackets and white gloves. It reminded me of what would be seen in the movies depicting the southern United States in the 1950s.

He began verbally assaulting and disrespecting many of the restaurant staff, which made me incredibly uncomfortable and angry. He then bragged about how he and some friends owned a fleet of trucks, which they used to distribute food and other types of aid donated by other countries. He further went on to say how they were able to scam and make a lot of money by exploiting everyone they could. By this time it took all of my self-control to not start punching this guy out.

I quickly finished my lunch and got out of there as fast as I could.

Unfortunately this would not be the first time I would see black people being treated unfairly during my time in Africa.

After lunch I found a bookstore and picked up a guidebook of Tanzania and quickly read it to become familiar with the country (as Tanzania had not been on my original itinerary).

After a couple of days in Zimbabwe, I made the short flight to Tanzania. After arriving I went to the hotel and met up with the other members of the tour. Some were from Canada, Australia, and Europe. I soon found out these people paid thousands of dollars in advance for this tour, I felt fortunate indeed that I had not.

We left the following morning in an oversized large military style open backed truck, which easily accommodated the group of twelve. Apparently, this tour would involve our sleeping in tents much of the time. I did not mind, as this was all part of the adventure.

As the days continued, we certainly were able to get up-close and personal with many wild animals. It was also reassuring to know that one of our guides always had a rifle on his shoulder if needed. I loved seeing the animals roaming around totally free. One late afternoon as the sun was beginning to set, we came across a male lion who was just strutting his stuff while slowly walking off into the distant sunset. It didn't get any cooler than that.

We arrived at our campsite later that night and were instructed to quickly set up our tents. It was totally dark by this time and we needed the headlights from the truck to help us see what we were doing. After our tents were up, our guide instructed us that under no circumstances were we to leave our tents during the night. There was a bathroom about fifty yards away, which we all made sure to visit before turning in for the night.

I remember lying in my tent and all of a sudden I could hear the sounds of lions roaring in the distance. Are you kidding me!? I couldn't believe it at first, but then understood why we were told not to leave our tents. Now here is the funny part. Here I am inside a nylon tent convincing myself I was safe and had all the protection I needed from being eaten alive by a den of lions out looking for a midnight buffet!! Needless to say I did survive the night, but being able to fall asleep was absolutely out of the question. The morning couldn't come soon enough and I remember getting out of my tent and looking to my left. I could not believe my eyes, seeing hundreds of zebras, wildebeests, and scattered giraffes no more than fifty yards from our campsite. What a beautiful yet surreal way to start one's morning.

The lions I had heard the night before certainly had their choice of dinner options and luckily human beings were not on their menus.

We left the campsite heading on to Kenya to visit a village of Masai warriors. (Their male rite of passage is to kill a lion single-handedly using only their spear). They were indeed brave people. We were told beforehand that if you wanted to take any photos of them you needed to ask permission first. Many in their culture still believed that if you took a photograph of them you were stealing their soul. As it turns out many of the tribe were happy to have their pictures taken. The going rate for this was five dollars, which we all gladly paid and knew it was helping them to financially survive.

We finally returned to our hotel in Tanzania. I had certainly seen all the animals I was hoping for, but decided to go out in the bush one more time on a private jeep tour.

Sitting in a range rover SUV was certainly a lot more comfortable than the back of the military style truck I had been on for ten days. As we drove through the countryside we suddenly came upon an elephant with her two babies walking behind her. About 200 yards behind them were three lions that were stalking them. We stopped our vehicle to watch how this would play out! (Yes, we were all rooting for the elephants!!) As the lions got closer, about 100 yards away, the mother elephant stopped in her tracks and quickly turned around and began charging the lions. (By the way, no matter what species you are talking about, you never mess with a mother's babies!) Those lions quickly retreated and ran off, never to be seen by us again. I have always thought that the lion was the king of the jungle, my experience that day taught me otherwise. You do not mess with elephants especially a mother elephant protecting her kids!!!

My time in Tanzania was more than I could have hoped for and I was grateful for this opportunity. Seeing the animals roaming free was inspiring. Now it was time for me to visit the northern border of Zimbabwe and the famous Victoria Falls.

Victoria Falls is an amazing place. My whitewater rafting experience on the Zambezi River beneath the falls is also highly recommended. Whenever I am out in nature and able to experience magnificent scenery, it always makes me feel closer to God. The sheer beauty and power of Victoria Falls was very inspiring to say the least. The whitewater rafting experience on the Zambezi River was full of pure adrenaline rushes if you like that sort of thing (I certainly do!). I took a few extra days to rest and soak up the magic of this place, and then moved on to South Africa before flying back to London to meet up with Anna.

My time in South Africa was split between the capital

Johannesburg and Cape Town. What a beautiful country, full of amazing things to see and do. This was April of 1993 and Apartheid and racial inequality and tension could be felt everywhere. I was never comfortable there because of this and hope and pray that life there now has improved for everybody.

Compared to Kenya, Tanzania, and even Zimbabwe, the infrastructure of South Africa was far superior. It is a beautiful country with much to see and experience. The city of Capetown is one of the most beautiful places on Earth. Everywhere you went to meet with people, the subject of racial inequality always came up. How could it not? This underlying current of unrest and tension was felt everywhere (at least by me), and hopefully in the last 25 years since I visited it has changed for the better.

Africa turned out to be a continent of great diversity and cultures. Seeing the animals on safari was interesting and at times exciting. I was now ready to head back to London and meet up with Anna. As incredible as my experiences with her were in Durango, I could only imagine what our trip to Israel and Egypt might be like.

I arrived in London one day before meeting with Anna and caught up on some much needed rest. I began to think about her Spiritual Teachers, mainly Jesus and Mother Mary. I also thought about my reading and her ability to contact her teachers at will, and how this might affect our trip to Israel and Egypt.

She arrived the next day and that evening we were on a plane headed for Israel. It was great to see her again and I shared more stories from my trip with her. Neither one of us had ever been to Israel or Egypt so we were both excited and looking forward to it.

Once in Israel we decided to go north and explore the area

around the Sea of Galilee first. With Anna's close connection to Jesus, she wanted to visit many of the places he traveled during his ministry. She also confided in me that she was one of the apostles during the time of Jesus (in a past life), which helped to explain her close connection with him. In time it was also revealed that I also had been one of his apostles during that time period. This new information helped me to better understand my connection with Anna, as well as to Jesus, Mother Mary and many other spiritual beings I would later be involved with.

We continued our tour of northern Israel, visiting Mount of Beatitudes where Jesus delivered his famous 'Sermon on the Mount'. The energy there felt very sacred, peaceful and loving as many people here were in deep prayer and contemplation. We next visited the Jordan River where Jesus was baptized. An area was marked where tour groups could safely enter the river to be baptized themselves. This river water was incredibly cold and I couldn't help but wonder if some of the people I observed were having a 'religious experience' or just freaking out because of the freezing water temperature. I am joking of course (or am I?).

After a few more days of exploring northern Israel we headed to the Holy city of Jerusalem. I couldn't wait to visit the 'old city' and especially the 'Western Wall', which in the Jewish faith is an extremely Holy site. It represents the last standing wall from the Holy temple built in 19 B.C. With my Jewish upbringing and yes, five years of Hebrew school, I was taught this Western Wall represented the Holiest site in Judaism. The Wall was a place where Jews from all over the world would come to pray and ask for blessings from God. Many people would even write down on paper what they prayed for, then roll it up and place it within the many crevices of the wall. I thought this would surely be a magical place and couldn't wait to visit it.

From our hotel to the walled off Old City of Jerusalem was a short walk. We immediately headed to the Jewish quarter so I could finally see and experience first hand the energy of the 'Western Wall.' Upon first seeing it from a distance, I began smiling and was more excited than ever to get even closer. Initially I was surprised to observe that about 80% of the wall was limited to men only and that women were given a much smaller area that they could visit. (That didn't seem to be very fair, but who am I to question?)

I entered the men's side and slowly walked up to the wall. I closed my eyes, raised my right arm and placed my hand directly on the wall. I don't know why I did this but I guess I was hoping for some type of religious experience. After a few seconds I heard a loud voice say in a very calm manner "IT'S ONLY A ROCK!!"

I quickly opened my eyes and noticed there wasn't anybody within fifty feet of me. I asked silently, who said that? I then heard the same voice say it is I, 'Lord Maitreya'. I was stunned and speechless once again. I remember hearing Lord Maitreya's name in one of Anna's classes, but did not really know who he was.

I began smiling to myself at his surprise message, wondering what it meant. As I left the wall area Anna was waiting for me and she noticed the stunned expression still on my face. She asked what happened and I shared my experience with her. She just smiled at me and said "they are trying to teach you." The they she was referring to are the Ascended Masters Teachers whom she and many others are consciously connected to and work with to help raise up humanity.

I asked her to further explain the message "it's only a rock"

which I had received while touching the Wall. She said Lord Maitreya came to you today because you are now ready to be taught the higher spiritual truths. His message was meant to convey to you that in order to see and understand the higher spiritual truths, you need to rise above all human and religious rhetoric. She explained that mankind through the ages had used religion to control and keep people in fear while distorting the truth about God. She said if I wanted to continue to grow spiritually I needed to release any and all religious doctrine I was still holding onto. Religion is man-made, not God-made. If religion was truly God-made, why are men and women not treated as equals in any of the organized religions? I couldn't argue with any of this, especially when I was looking at the discrepancy of the Wall access for men and women here in Israel.

I felt the need to sit down for a minute to process what I had just been told and experienced. I felt another big shift take place within me, and realized how being in such a Spiritual magic place with Anna was helping me open up even more to greater spiritual awareness and possibilities. I will say one thing for sure; I will never again look at the 'Western Wall' without remembering those words "it's only a rock."

One other lesson from this day was that humankind can place their religious values and beliefs in any specific person, place or thing, but the Higher Spiritual truth is that God exists in everything (not just holy sites) and in everything exists God. Yes, the Western Wall holds a deeply religious symbology for many people, but from the perspective of an Ascended Master, apparently it's JUST A ROCK! (I do not mean to be disrespectful in any way towards organized religions, I only ask that you keep an open mind and open heart to what I am sharing with you and what I was told.)

My experience at the wall seemed to raise the energy of our trip and set the stage for more interactions with Anna's guides. Next we entered the Christian quarter of the old city and went directly to the Church of the Holy Sepulcher, the place where many believe Jesus was crucified and also buried.

As we entered the church, Anna said that Jesus was here with us now and communicating with her. (I thought, it doesn't get any better than this!) He began by explaining that many of the religious sites in the 'old city' are just approximations of where the actual events took place. He then asked us to find a seat and take a moment to bless and surround this church and all who enter it in his Pure White Light. Continuing to sit in the church, we noticed several religious processions (from the many different factions which occupy and control the different areas of this sacred church). Each faction had their own burning incense and as the subsequent smoke filled the air, it appeared each group was marking its territorial rights within the church. I could only think that Jesus was looking down on this shaking his head and saying really!! In my opinion there is no room for politics in any aspect of Faith and God.

We made it a point to visit this church every day while in Jerusalem and blessing it like Jesus had requested. Even though I was raised in the Jewish tradition, I always felt comfortable when Jesus or any of Anna's guides came in to share information with us. As our trip continued I was constantly talking to them through her, always asking many questions. Fortunately for me they did not seem to mind. I thought to myself how cool is this having Jesus, Mother Mary and many others serving as our personal tour guides?

As we continued exploring the old city, Anna's guides were always with us. Having them around all the time gave me a real sense of safety and being totally protected no matter what was going on around us. She said her guides are always close even when she is home, and she got a kick out of how excited I was about them hanging out with us so much. Wherever we went we were being given information and insight into the true nature and history of this remarkable place. I cannot fully explain how it felt being in the Presence and Energy of these Amazing Beings of Light, but I sure liked it!

After exploring Jerusalem we headed south to visit Masada. For some reason I wanted to be at the top of this mountain for sunrise, so Anna and I got an early start and hiked up to the top of the mountain. About an hour later we were rewarded with one of the most spectacular sunrises coming up from the desert I had ever seen. (Interestingly enough, years later they installed a tram like at Disneyworld, which gets you to the top in five minutes.)

It was then off to float in the Dead Sea, a very unique opportunity due to the high salt concentration. I definitely recommend Masada and the Dead Sea to anyone visiting Israel. Israel proved to be a very rewarding experience for both of us. Regardless of your religious or spiritual background, Israel is a fascinating place to visit and I have been blessed to visit there many times over the years. It is interesting to note that each time I have visited it has been a unique experience. All my experiences there have taught me that the majority of the people just want to live in peace with each other and enjoy their families and be free to practice the religion of their choice. It was now time to fly to Cairo, Egypt and go explore the pyramids.

Cairo is a very busy but interesting place. It is the only place I have ever been where the drivers turn a three lane highway into a five lane highway by overlapping the lane lines on the road. I admit after I got used to this I became impressed with the ingenuity and choreography involved to pull this off.

The pyramids were better than expected. Until you physically stand next to them you cannot fully appreciate their massive size and prefect geometry. After seeing the size of the individual stones I could not envision how these were cut, molded and placed with such precision by human beings alone. (A subject for another time perhaps?)

As Anna and I walked around the sphinx on the Gaza plateau, she suddenly stopped and said, "I see many rooms not yet discovered under the sphinx which contain medical technology that will be used in the future." She explained very advanced civilizations had previously existed on earth and that much of the technology has been preserved until mankind can once again accept it without trying to manipulate it for destructive purposes. When will humankind ever learn?

Another group of pyramids existed about 12 miles south of Giza at Sakkara. I decided to ride horses there through the desert as Anna wisely chose to return to our hotel. As my guide and I traveled south through the desert on our individual horses, I felt like I was in a Lawrence of Arabia movie. These horses were incredibly strong and fast and we reached Sakkara quickly. I gladly got off my horse to give my body, especially my backside, a small break. The intensity of the sun and the wind blowing sand in my face was an interesting way to spend an afternoon. After a short break, it was time to get back on the horses and head back to Giza.

I will never forget how fast those horses ran once they knew they were heading back to their stables. I was holding on with all my strength, at the same laughing about what a crazy idea this had been. We finally reached the stables with all my body parts still intact, so all in all this had been another great day. Flying through the desert on such amazing horses and amazing scenery is something I and my posterior will never forget!! I also remember that walking and sitting for the next few days was indeed a challenge in itself (the things we do when we are younger and dumber).

After a few more days in Egypt it was time for Anna to return home. Our time together had been fun and I enjoyed the energy, information and company her amazing Teachers and Guides provided us on this journey. When I returned to the states after a short trip through the Greek islands I promised I would call her.

My time in the beautiful Greek islands went quickly. If you ever have the opportunity to visit the Island of Santorini, it should definitely be added to your bucket list. The islands of Mykonos, and Rhodes were also quite interesting and scenic in their own right.

After a couple of weeks visiting Athens and many other Greek islands I was once again feeling tired and decided to end my trip early and return to the states.

After returning home, I spoke with Anna and told her I had one more short trip I wanted to take. I wanted to walk the Inca trail in Peru to visit the ruins at Macchu Picchu and experience a Ayahuasca ceremony with a Peruvian Shaman. I originally signed up for a tour with some friends but it had been canceled due to not enough people signing up for it.

I was determined to go anyway, and ended up hiring the same guide and cook the tour group would have used. After resting for a few weeks in Florida it was soon time to leave for Peru.

Upon arriving in Cusco, Peru, the departure point for Macchu Picchu, I spent three days acclimating myself to the high altitude. It was finally the day to depart and after a short bus ride, myself, the guide and the cook set out to begin the hike on the Inca trail.

The next four days involved strenuous hiking and some of the most awesome mountain trails and terrain I have ever seen. Unlike the Himalayan Mountains in Nepal, the mountains in Peru were much greener and more inviting, in my opinion. While on some of the dramatic narrow hiking trails I felt like I was walking directly in the heart of Mother Earth.

I got lost in thought in these amazing mountains and was sadly disappointed when the hike was over and we arrived at our destination, the ruins of Macchu Picchu. Some people say the journey can sometimes be more fulfilling than the final destination, and that was definitely true for me here. The days on the Inca Trail were truly magical and the energy was intoxicating. Now don't get me wrong, the ruins at Macchu Picchu are well worth visiting, but for me the journey getting there was more spiritually uplifting and fulfilling.

The last thing on my itinerary before leaving Peru was to visit a shaman (a traditional medicine man) and experience an Ayahuasca ceremony under his guidance and supervision. This ceremony involves the drinking of a plant mixture which affects your level of consciousness and is used for healing and religious purposes in many South American countries. This should always be administered by an experienced Shaman to ensure it is a safe process.

My guides and a friend of theirs who had previously worked with the shaman all boarded a large truck for the 5-hour drive into the jungle. I did not know what to expect but trusted my guides that I was once again in safe hands.

After arriving at our destination we immediately went to meet up with the Shaman. He welcomed us into his hut and started scanning us individually with his eyes, apparently to determine if we were good candidates to partake in his

Ceremony. Through my interpreter he asked if I had ever drank the ayahuasca before and I replied no. He then had me sit in a chair as he performed some type of cleansing ritual which apparently cleared me to participate.

Soon thereafter he gave each of us a carefully measured glass of liquid to drink. Within a few minutes I could feel energy shooting out through the top of my head. I was instructed to lie down and just relax. In time, colored images began to flood my mind almost like watching a movie in technicolor. I could hear the Shaman chanting, I opened my eyes and saw him waving his arms around us as if he were cleansing our bodies. I don't know how long this went on but I eventually fell asleep and awoke the following morning.

We ate breakfast with him and then he had us go outside and plant some seeds in his garden, as a way of thanking and blessing Mother Earth (similar to what the Native American Indians do in their culture).

Then through my interpreter, he began to tell me about my father who had been back in spirit for about seven years. That blew my mind a little, but I was getting more used to these kinds of experiences. I then thanked him for my healing and the Sacred Ceremony. Before I left, I gave him one of my green surgical shirts and he responded by giving me one of his Ceremonial shirts made from tree bark. We had both exchanged the shirts we had done our respective healing in, and exchanged a warm hug. I felt a strong connection with him and thought this was a great way to end my year long travels. I once again felt grateful for this experience and human connection.

I left Peru feeling complete and would now return to the states to figure out what I would do next.

My original intent for doing all this traveling was not only to experience new places, people and things, but to learn more about myself as well. I believe I was successful in doing all of that. I had been to a lot of places, experienced a lot of things, but what stands out most in my mind are all the heart-to-heart human connections I made along the way.

I learned that all human beings are truly connected to each other regardless of culture, language or geographical location. I wish more people would get that memo so they would treat each other with more kindness and respect.

I was definitely grateful for the opportunity to do these trips, but I now felt a deeper sense of purpose with regards to Anna, her guides and teachers and definitely the Future Cities of Light.

I had had my time to play, for which I was very grateful, and was now ready to begin the next chapter of my life.

Chapter Nine

My New Life in Durango
(Graduate School is Now in Session!!)

Returning home to south Florida, I took a few weeks to rest and recuperate from my trip to Peru. It had been a year since I began the first leg of my trip throughout Southeast Asia, and I couldn't believe how fast the time went. It was now the fall of 1993 and time for me to look at my future.

I remained in close contact with Anna, and suggested to her my strong interest in the Cities of Light. After a short period, she got back to me and said with her Teacher's approval, she was now inviting me to come live with her in Durango, Colorado to begin my Spiritual training.

I moved to Durango soon after that, and once again immediately felt the magic of this place. Before I moved there however, Anna said I would have to cut all ties with my friends in order to be totally focused on my training. With all I had seen and experienced on my first trip in Durango, as well as on our trip to Israel and Egypt, this was a relatively easy decision to make. To be trained first hand by Jesus, Mother Mary, St. Germain, Archangel Michael, and many others was an overwhelming opportunity and blessing I could not pass up. I hoped my friends would be able to understand some day the opportunity I was being given.

Anna continued to teach her weekly meditation classes as well as facilitate a monthly rebirthing workshop. All her Teachers were at every event she hosted and did much work on all who chose to participate. The energy during those sessions was very powerful and healing at the same time.

At the monthly rebirthing event, she explained it was a powerful cleansing process using rapid deep breathing techniques. With the help of her Teachers, people were quickly able to release emotional, physical, and mental negative experiences past and present. By having these blockages removed one could feel emotionally lighter and happier, and experience more clarity within their own lives. I loved doing these rebirthings because they were so powerful and healing. This is a very unique experience and is different each time you do one, depending on what issues are brought to the surface for you. I strongly recommend you try one if you ever have the opportunity.

One day Anna and I were talking and I made the comment, I know who your Teachers are, but who are mine? She explained that since we were "Twin Rays" (two beings sharing the same Soul Light and Energy) that her Teachers were my teachers as well. This helped further explain why I always felt so comfortable around Anna and her Teachers. (I will now refer to her Teachers as our Teachers.)

Just as in my experience with Anna in Israel and Egypt, our Teachers were around us constantly. They were always offering us information, guidance and protection. What a blessing to be able to spend so much time in their loving energy.

Since Anna and I had both worked with Jesus in past lives, and because we were also "Twin Rays," Jesus strongly encouraged her to take me under her wing and train me. He said we would both work in the "City of Light" together and that our combined energies would allow us to help and serve many. I was excited to hear all this, but quickly learned I had a lot of work to do on myself before reaching that point.

Our first few months together were difficult for both of us. Anna could see right through me and was constantly exposing all my faults and weaknesses. (By the way, just for the record, we all have them, that's what makes us human.) These flaws are human ego personality traits we have learned and acquired based on our life experiences past and present. At first I would get angry with her when she pointed these things out. I soon realized she was trying to help me get rid of my human ego personality junk. She said if I wanted to do the spiritual work at the City that I had to release this stuff because it no longer served me. This is not a comfortable process to go through, but if you are lucky enough to have someone in your life to do this for you it is a blessing indeed. By acknowledging our own human faults and weaknesses (or having someone do it for us) is the only way we can overcome them and become stronger.

Releasing our own ego personality flaws and emotional garbage is a necessary but uncomfortable part of being on one's spiritual path to enlightenment. We must first learn to see truth about ourselves, before we can see the truth in others and truly be of service to them. At times Anna became impatient with me, but Jesus was always there to help smooth things over. It's interesting how stubborn and set in our ways the human ego can be. I found the rebirthing sessions to be a very powerful and rapid way to release a lot of this emotional garbage and I always felt so much lighter and happier afterwards.

As time went by, I became much less resistant and much more accepting of what Anna and our Teachers were teaching and showing me about myself. They would explain where some of my behavior patterns came from and instructed me how to release them. At times I felt totally exposed and vulnerable, but was determined to work through it no matter how uncomfortable or painful it was. I felt honored to be hand picked to do this incredible spiritual work, and there was no way I was going to disappoint my Teachers or Anna. Anna was incredibly strict with me at the beginning and I am glad she was, because I needed it.

When I mentioned in the title of this chapter that graduate school was now in session I wasn't kidding. Just like in military boot camp when the participants are broken down and then built back up, I was going through my own spiritual boot camp experience and process. In time, thanks to the patience, guidance, and love and support from Anna and my Beloved Teachers, I was able to achieve a certain level of humility and inner peace. These two attributes are mandatory for anyone trying to achieve a higher level of spiritual understanding and consciousness. Until we become Ascended Masters, this process of growth, self-examination and self-correction is ongoing for each of us!!!

As I continued to learn and grow it was now time for me to learn how to communicate with our Teachers as Anna could. I remember one afternoon she instructed me to lie on the living room floor, close my eyes and begin breathing deeply. She eventually led me up into "God's Garden" as she always did in her meditation class. After awhile she began asking me if I could see or hear anyone. I initially said no, but soon felt an overwhelming wave of Pure Love and Energy, which brought tears to my eyes. I said I believe Jesus is here with me now, and she immediately said "very good, he is here now!" This was the first time I had ever truly felt his Love and Light (at least in this lifetime!) and I tell you it was life changing. Whatever religious doctrines of my Jewish upbringing that may still have existed within me were immediately dissolved and released that day.

I was inspired by that experience and Anna genuinely seemed pleased at my progress. As time went on she would continue to have me meditate and then question me on who I was seeing, hearing, or feeling. The main teachers we were working with were Jesus, Mother Mary, St. Germain, Archangel Michael, Lord Maitreya, and Commander Ashtar.

I was becoming more and more comfortable doing this and with practice was soon able to differentiate the different energy of each Teacher. Anna was always there supervising and encouraging me to keep practicing. At the same time my Teachers were also incredibly loving, nurturing, and supportive. It is interesting to note that just like each human being has their own unique energy and vibration, so do the Beloved Ascended Masters. Having them around us so much of the time always made us feel safe and protected and definitely blessed.

I continued to take advantage of the weekly meditation classes and monthly rebirthings and was pleased with the growth and progress I was making. One night, while Anna and I were getting ready to leave for meditation class, she decided she was not feeling well enough to lead the class and she told me I would have to do it. She stayed home to rest as I left for the church to lead the class that night. At first I felt a little apprehensive about doing this but before I left the house she reassured me that I was more than capable.

I arrived at the church feeling confident knowing our Teachers would be there to participate as they always were for Anna. The class went off without a hitch, and I even channeled a message for the group just like Anna always did. I felt a real sense of accomplishment that night and a heightened sense of confidence in working with my Teachers. After I returned home Anna asked how things went. (I knew she already had the answer from her teachers.) I replied all went well and that I had a lot of fun leading the class. She then said, "See how far you've come in such a short period of time." I smiled and said thank you.

Easter of 1994 was quickly approaching and Anna decided to do a special channeling event at the church on Easter Sunday. What I am about to say might sound strange to you, but she said "God the Father" had agreed to come channel through her on Easter Sunday and give a special message to the group. I had never in all the books I read ever heard of anyone doing this. Was God really going to make an appearance in Durango, Colorado on Easter Sunday 1994? I had been with Anna long enough now to never question or doubt her abilities. If she said the Father told her he would do this for her that was more than good enough for me!

In the meantime I shared this information with my brother Allan in Detroit, and he quickly made travel plans to come and witness this event in person. He had never met Anna and was more than curious. His business partner at that time also decided to make the trip.

The big day had finally arrived and the church was full to overflowing. One of the members of Anna's meditation class agreed to video this event. You could feel the excitement and anticipation of everyone in the church that day.

Anna was sitting center stage dressed in white and I was sitting just to her left (as I always did) about three feet away. My brother and his business partner were sitting in the second row and I am sure neither one of them was quite sure what to expect.

Before the event even started, my brother's partner (who by the way was raised in an orthodox Jewish family) saw Jesus standing directly behind Anna and apparently Jesus winked at him. How would he explain that to his rabbi, I thought later on, laughing to myself.

It was now time to begin, as Anna closed her eyes awaiting the entrance of "God the Father" to arrive. As she continued sitting quietly with her eyes closed, suddenly her body began to tremble. I had seen her channel numerous times before but never saw her body shake like this. This continued for about ten more minutes and then all of a sudden I felt a jolt of energy slam me into the back of my chair. It felt like someone took the palm of their hand, placed it on my chest and thrust me backwards. I was definitely startled, for I had never felt such a power before. It certainly got my attention and is something I will never forget.

Soon after I experienced that jolt of "God Energy," Anna's body stopped trembling and she began to speak. The Father first explained how he had to dial down his energy to make it as comfortable as possible for Anna. It still took her a while for her to be able to hold the energy but she seemed more comfortable with it now. He then began to bless the group, as well as give personal messages to many who were in attendance. The whole time he was speaking, the room was full of such Love and Power unlike anything I had ever felt. He spoke a lot about love that day and how he wished all his children on earth would love, respect, and treat each other better.

As I was sitting within three feet of Anna watching her do this, I was completely in awe of what was actually occurring. At one point she opened her eyes to look at the group and I could definitely see those eyes were not hers, as she seemed totally transformed.

Afterwards on the recorded video you could actually see the "Father's Face" overshadowing hers, including her eyes. If that doesn't give somebody the chills, nothing ever will.

As she continued to scan her head around the room she then looked directly into my eyes and I felt the Father's Love and Power go right through me. As I looked into her eyes, there was no question in my mind that the Father was overshadowing her and I had goosebumps on my arms to prove it. She then closed her eyes, the Father once again Blessed all in attendance and then He was gone.

Anna slowly opened her eyes and it took her at least ten minutes before she could ground herself and refocus back into the energy of the room. I was so proud of her. When it came to all things spiritual she was absolutely fearless, and always ready to be of service even if it meant trying something new and difficult. Her Faith in God and all our Teachers was truly on display this day.

The church and all the people were still buzzing about what just occurred. The energy in that room was at an all time high. Anna slowly came back and appeared somewhat intoxicated. (Can you blame her?) She could not remember much of what occurred that day and was excited to watch the video.

My brother's reaction to this event was interesting. Remember, this was his first time seeing Anna do her spiritual work. He later shared his experience. He said "I could feel the power, energy and Love of the Father fill the church," and he admitted it was a little frightening. He couldn't believe Anna could channel and hold the energy of God the way she did. He certainly would never look at Anna in the same light again. He had a new respect for her abilities and power. (To tell the truth, so did I!)

I know many people reading this may have a hard time believing what had happened that day. I am here to tell you that I definitely felt that "God Force" push me back into my chair. I definitely looked into Anna's eyes and knew it was not her speaking or seeing. I also saw the video with "God's Face" overshadowing and transforming hers. Wow! What a day for all who were blessed enough to experience that event first hand.

Time seemed to fly by as we continued to wait for further information on the geographical location for the "City of Light" we were to open. These "Cities of Light" were going to be amazing places for healing, education, and the arts. They were going to be places where the Ascended Masters would materialize for all to see and be able to interact with. These Cities will also be closely monitored by the Ascended Masters, to ensure that human ego does not come into play to bring them down as in the ancient cities of Atlantis and Lemuria.

There have been many advanced civilizations throughout Earth's history which were eventually destroyed because humankind chose to use advanced technology for destructive purposes. Just imagine what life would be like on planet Earth today if we were as spiritually advanced as we are technologically. I strongly believe in time this will be so.

With my interest and background in medicine, I was anxious to learn more about future healing. One night during meditation class I was again taken to visit with the doctor on the ship. He explained some of the healing in the future will involve "electron manipulation." If you remember from high school chemistry (yes, I can hear you all groaning now!) an atom consists of a nucleus in the center containing neutrons and protons surrounded by electrons. (Please do not worry, there will not be a test!) The electrons whirl around the nucleus and are what allows atoms to bond to each other forming matter. In other words, electrons are the glue which holds atoms together. This is an oversimplified explanation but it's the only one I can understand.

It was further explained to me that if someone has a broken bone, and you are able to manipulate and increase the speed of the electrons in the cells responsible for bone healing, that spontaneous healing could be accomplished. (Sounds crazy, right?) If someone has a tumor in their body and you could stop the electron movement completely in the tumor cells, the tumor would dissolve. Again, this is a very basic explanation to what is probably a very complex process. You know some people say we only use 10% of our brain, maybe in the other 90% is the more detailed explanation of how this future healing will work. Either way I am excited to learn this new technology. Anything that can help cure or prevent further human pain and suffering is something I want to be part of.

Anna and I kept asking questions about the "City of Light" location and finally were instructed to relocate to southeastern Arizona. We were both excited for this new opportunity and left Durango in the summer of 1996.

Chapter Ten

When the Student Becomes the Teacher

Upon arriving in southeastern Arizona, all we could think about was the "City of Light" and where it might be located. Our Teachers had instructed us to move here and we hoped that meant it would soon be time for us to find the property and begin construction. In the meantime I went and met the local hospital administrator who was very much interested in me practicing podiatric medicine and surgery in the community. I was offered an office directly across the street from the hospital and would have been the only full-time podiatrist in town at that time. It was a very tempting offer, but our Teachers said we probably wouldn't be in this specific area long enough and recommended I not take it. This was the summer of 1996 and all signs pointed to the "City of Light" which would require all our time and effort.

As it turned out, plans for the city were delayed so we decided to do some more traveling. We went back to Israel and Egypt a few more times as well as England and parts of Europe.

During one of our trips to England, we hired a driver and went to the countryside outside of London looking for crop circles. Crop circles are geometrical patterns that appear usually in wheat or cornfields. Some of these are definitely man-made while others may have another source for their creation. (I will leave that decision up to you and your belief system.) We had our driver take us to the small town of Avebury, which had a history of having crop circles appearing quite frequently. We stopped at a small bookshop there and they gave us directions to a newly discovered crop circle just out of town.

We followed their directions and suddenly in the distance we saw a woman dressed in white waving her arms to get our attention. We stopped the car, got out and started walking towards where we saw the woman waving her arms at us. Sure enough, we soon came upon a beautiful crop circle, but the woman in white was nowhere to be seen. We started laughing and just assumed she was an angel who materialized briefly to show us the location of the crop circle. Things like this happened frequently for us and it always made us laugh. By the way, as I was walking in to the center of the crop circle my video camera was experiencing some type of electro-magnetic interference, which later showed up as horizontal white lines on the videotape. This evidence made me think that this was not a man-made crop circle after all. Nonetheless, without help from our Lady in White, we would never have found the field in the first place.

On another trip we were visiting the beautiful Greek island of Santorini. Our cruise boat anchored off shore and we were shuttled back and forth by smaller boats. On our return back to the cruise ship the water was very rough, with about four to six foot waves. As our shuttle boat tied up to the big ship I very carefully jumped off first with the help of multiple crewmembers. Anna was now still on the shuttle boat as I was facing her with my arms extended standing on the cruise ship. The waves continued to really rock that smaller boat making it dangerous for her to attempt to get off yet. All of a sudden I hear Anna say "Michael (referring to Archangel Michael), you get down here now and stop this boat from rocking!" In a very surreal couple of seconds the waves stopped, she comfortably jumped off and was now safely with me aboard the cruise ship. As soon as she was safely off the shuttle boat the high waves resumed, much to the dismay of my brother who was behind Anna and still on the small boat. He said "Hey, what about me!" I will never forget the wide-eyed looks on the crewmembers' faces as the waves just suddenly stopped so Anna could safely disembark. It was as if everything was moving in slow motion and then quickly sped up again. It still makes me laugh to this day when I think about it. Oh, by the way, my brother did get off the boat safely, still wondering why Michael didn't stop the waves from rocking the boat for him. I fondly refer to this incident as the day the boat stood still.

It become second nature to have our Teachers and other Angelic Beings around us and always helping us in whatever way they could. Sometimes it was funny how they could just manipulate time and space like Archangel Michael did for Anna on the day the boat stood still. On our travels and in our daily life together Anna and I never knew what could happen or what to expect from our Teachers. This always made for a lot of fun and interesting experiences.

There was also the time when we were visiting Fatima, Portugal (the place where Mother Mary physically materialized to three shepherd children in 1917, delivering messages to them). We were sitting in the open-air chapel and Mother Mary began communicating with both of us at the same time. She was telling us she spends much of Her time in Fatima helping and healing many. I had never visited a holy site where you could feel so much love in the air. By the way if you ever start smelling the fragrance of red roses and you are not around any flowers, Mother Mary may be paying you a visit. She does this a lot for people, it is kind of Her calling card. To be able to visit and experience Fatima along with having a visit from Mother Mary was a priceless blessing indeed.

As the years flew by, we were still waiting for the time to begin our work at the New City. Anna would constantly remind me that things would happen in God's time, not ours! Patience is something I never was good at when I was younger, but have gotten much better at through the years. Although I never liked hearing her repeated message, I knew it was the truth and had to accept it.

Our Teachers explained that part of the delay was due to "Divine Timing", and in order to bring the "Cities of Light" through also had to do with the level of Spiritual Consciousness of the planet. The Spiritual Hierarchy, who oversee planet Earth, decided to give humankind more time to exercise their free will and become more spiritually awakened. (I sure was hoping this would happen soon)!

I was taught that time doesn't exist in the higher dimensions of reality as it does here on earth. A blink of an eye in the higher dimensions could be twenty years or even much more of earth time. Rarely do Ascended Masters make date and time predictions because time for them is much more fluid and because they always have to account for and respect human free will. You would be surprised to know how powerful human free will plays out in our reality here on earth.

Anna and I continued to wait patiently (or sometimes not so much), and we were given permission to continue traveling, which we did. It was now the beginning of 2006 and we had been living in Arizona for almost ten years. It truly is amazing how fast time can go by at different stages in our life. When we are younger we want time to speed up, and when we are older we want it to slow down. The truth is, time is a constant in our third dimension. How we perceive it and our level of consciousness are the variables constantly changing.

One morning Anna woke up and was having a difficult time swallowing, which also affected her breathing. I was concerned and took her to the emergency room for treatment. After that, her condition continued to get worse and she was also experiencing muscle weakness in her legs making it more difficult for her to walk. She also started having some difficulty talking, as her speech began to slur sometimes. After further testing and evaluation she was diagnosed with ALS (Amyotrophic Lateral Sclerosis), also commonly referred to as Lou Gehrig's disease, (named after a famous baseball player who had this disease). This is a neuro-muscular disease, which affects nerve cells in the brain and spinal cord. With this disease nerve cells are prevented from sending impulses to the muscles to make them function. Without these vital nerve communications our muscles simply cannot work. There is still no cure for this and it affects about 30,000 people in the United States alone.

This rapid change in Anna's health seemed surreal to both of us. After all we had seen and experienced with our Spiritual Guides and Teachers, and the work yet to be done at the future "Cities of Light," this just didn't make sense on a third dimensional level of understanding. We were later told that Anna had agreed to take on this disease (not on a conscious level but by her higher oversoul). But we were not told if she was going to be given a miracle cure.

As the weeks went by, her condition continued to deteriorate. Swallowing, breathing, eating, talking and even walking became a challenge for her. She did make me promise that I would not take her back to the hospital, no matter what. I reluctantly agreed and took care of her in any way I could. All during this time she was able to maintain a positive attitude and never complained about her condition even once. Her faith, strength and courage were incredibly inspiring to me, as I always thought in the back of my mind that our Teachers would come and heal her.

One day we were talking and she said Jesus came and told her he was coming for her soon. I then asked is he coming to heal you or take you back to spirit? She replied I do not know.

Within two weeks of her receiving that message, she woke up one day with both feet and ankles severely swollen. I knew this meant her organs were beginning to shut down. I asked her if she wanted to go to the hospital, she said absolutely not and just smiled at me. It was now July 2006 and she had been battling this for about six months.

The next afternoon we were talking and suddenly she just slumped over in her chair losing consciousness. I picked her up and put her to bed. I then put my fingers in both her hands and told her to squeeze if she could hear me. There was no response from her and I immediately knew she was beginning her transition out of her physical body back into the spirit world. All of my years of training with her suddenly kicked in and I was as supportive as possible.

The room was now full of Angels and all our Teachers, including Jesus. They were there to help and support us both as Anna was going through her transition process. This was my first time being with someone as they transitioned. If you ever find yourself in this position it is very important to be as loving and supportive as you can. This will make it a more peaceful process for your loved one. The last thing they need to deal with during this time are highly emotional people around them. This just makes it much more difficult for them to concentrate and focus on what they need to do for themselves. Yes, they can hear what is going on around them, so you can speak to them if you wish. I gently thanked her for all she did for me in this lifetime and knew she was in good hands with all the Beings of Light in the room. Many people believe if you practice meditation on a regular basis that when it comes time for your transition, it will be quite easy because you have already practiced and experienced leaving your body.

As her transition process continued, the peace and love felt in that room was soothing to me and I am sure to her as well. When you believe in reincarnation as I do, then you know you will see your loved one again. This made it easier for me to release my emotional ties to her so she could transition more readily. I believe when our Soul leaves the physical body it is just changing zip codes, so to speak, and goes to reside in a different plane or dimension of reality. The fact that Anna and I are "Twin Rays" and will continue to work together regardless of what side of the veil she resides on, also made this a little easier for me to deal with.

I could feel our Teacher's overshadowing presence over both of us the whole time. This is the only explanation I have for how I was able to remain so calm. Eventually she took her last breath and simultaneously a tear from her right eye ran down the side of her face. That was her way of saying goodbye.

Her Soul had completed the transition from her physical form and I was happy she was no longer suffering. The energy of the room quickly changed as the Beings of Light escorted her Soul back to the higher dimensions, where we both reside in between human incarnations. I now gave myself permission to cry and release, which I did before doing anything else.

I immediately thought about my father's passing some twenty years earlier when I had no spiritual knowledge of how third dimensional physical death really worked. My knowledge now would be a great comfort and strength as I moved forward.

The truth is we are all spiritual beings having a physical experience on earth, not the other way around. If we were physical beings having a spiritual experience, wouldn't we then take our physical forms with us when we left?

Before I forget, I want to recommend an excellent book titled *The Mystery of Death and Dying* by Earlyne Chaney. This book goes into extreme detail explaining the Soul's exit from the body during physical death.

After years of reading, studying and then being trained under Anna and our Beloved Teachers, I know that each one of our Souls is IMMORTAL, because our Soul represents our own individual God Creation and Connection and that never ends!

It was now time for me to re-focus and deal with the third dimensional responsibilities regarding Anna's physical death. I phoned 911 and within minutes my house was swarming with paramedics, firemen, and police (God bless these first responders for all that they do to be of service). I was still somewhat in shock and my house was now full of strangers. It all seemed a little surreal to me. Soon everyone was gone, the people from the funeral home removed her body and I found myself just sitting there totally alone and exhausted. I was physically, mentally, and emotionally drained. The last six months of taking care of her had finally caught up to me. At least I now had my Spiritual knowledge and training, and more importantly, my Beloved Spiritual Guides and Teachers to keep me strong and balanced moving forward.

I remember waking up the next day and going into meditation. It was hard to stay focused but I did the best I could. I rededicated myself that morning to all my Spiritual

Teachers, that I would spend the rest of this lifetime doing the work Anna had done, including working toward the "City of Light" and being of Service. I have never felt as determined or committed as I did that day, and that feeling has never diminished, it just continues to grow within me.

Now with the full support of my Teachers, I, the student, was now thrust into being the teacher. I felt more than ready to do my part in being of service and in helping as many people as I could, just like Anna did. That was the least I could do in honoring her life and all our Beloved Teachers, and of course God.

The Fire-Walking Foot Doctor

Chapter Eleven

Time to Spiritually Reinvent Myself

As I returned home from Anna's funeral, I want to share one of my experiences with you. I was at the cemetery, parked in my rental car directly behind the hearse, awaiting the burial ceremony. As I was looking at her casket through the back window of the hearse, I heard her voice as clear as day say, "I'm not in here, I'm with you!" Over the years I have heard many messages and was no longer surprised or startled by them. Her message brought me some much needed comfort on a rather difficult day. Her message was just another example that one's consciousness continues onward even after physical death.

She taught me in life, as she taught me in her third dimensional death/transition, to always be strong but humble, courageous, but silent (unless called upon to do the "Father's work) and never to complain. She also literally stamped on my forehead to always acknowledge and give thanks to where the real power comes from in all things, Father/Mother God. This was especially important when facilitating classes or doing any healing work. We are just the vessels our Teachers use to shine their divine energy through us in order to do the work.

It was now time for me to continue on my spiritual path without her by my side, at least not physically. She continues to this day to support me, especially when I am doing my spiritual work. I used the additional time I now had to continue reading, studying and learning. I also continue to facilitate rebirthing and meditation classes whenever possible.

Unfortunately, there is a lot of ego in the third dimensional spiritual community today, but I want you to remember one thing. Spirituality is not a competition or a race, it is a journey (a never-ending one, no matter what dimension you reside in). We are all at different stages of our spiritual advancement, so be not concerned with what others are doing, focus on yourself instead.

Just as there are no two people on earth with identical fingerprints (think about the creative God Intelligence that could accomplish that with the approximately six to seven billion people here now!), no two people have the exact same life experiences either. We are all unique souls with our own lessons to learn, things to experience and karma to work out. No two snowflakes are identical yet they share water as their common source. No two human beings are exactly identical yet they share the same source as well, the Father/Mother Universal Supreme God. This is what connects us all and makes us all part of one family. If more people understood this and truly believed it, think how much better our world would be today.

There is an old saying that "God comforts the disturbed and disturbs the comfortable." When we are going through tough times we get the help and comfort we need. When we get too comfortable and lazy, our soul pushes us out of our comfort zone to take on new lessons and resume our personal growth.

I want to bring up another important topic I previously touched upon briefly and that is the role of "Free Will" in our lives. Each soul in embodiment or in spirit for that matter is given the gift of free will. Free will allows us to make decisions both good and bad, which serve as lessons for our soul's

148

journey. God has created us and given us free will so that we can learn and grow in our own space and time. When we have reached certain levels of spiritual attainment we are trusted with greater and greater powers and abilities with which to help those around us. If we misuse these they are quickly taken away from us. Without free will, how would we ever be tested to see if we learned our lessons?

The "Mighty Masters" and "Beings of Light" are always offering their Love, Wisdom and Power in order to help us, but we have to ask for their assistance first. The law of free will is a "Divine Law" and even the "Great Ascended Masters" must respect it. In other words, we must invite them into our lives, which gives them permission to help us. Otherwise they usually cannot intercede on our behalf because of human free will. There are exceptions to this, but for the most part learn to ask for help and make sure you are receptive to accepting their blessings. The Beloved Teachers and Guides observe us always, hoping we make the right choices.

How often in our lives have we done something that we knew and felt wasn't quite right for us, but went ahead and did it anyway? (So how did that work out for you?) If we learn to listen to our inner voice or even trust our gut, it can help us prevent making mistakes and bad choices. We all make mistakes and bad choices at different times in our lives, but it is important to always learn from these and try NOT to repeat the same ones over and over. After all, we are still residing in the human 3rd dimension and are far from perfect, so learn to forgive yourself and others when mistakes are made. Easier said than done, but at least try.

Being on my own again after so many years of living with Anna took time for me to adjust. I continued my daily spiritual meditation and practice, something I strongly recommend for everyone. The power of developing your own self-discipline by adhering to a daily spiritual practice of some kind can really help keep you balanced and grounded.

Many spiritual disciplines teach us to try and live in the Now, the present. To not let our emotions get too high or too low in our day-to-day existence. This is not easy to do, as our past memories and future expectations can often flood our mind and thoughts. In my experience meditation is a very powerful tool to help you stay more grounded and in the present. Yesterday is gone and tomorrow never gets here, so all we really have is right now! In my opinion there is no right or wrong way to meditate. Just find some technique that works for you and try incorporating it into your daily routine. Meditation forces the mind to slow down and the body to relax, and is a great way to reduce stress. If you are in a Ferrari sports car speeding down the highway at 150 miles an hour everything around you looks like a blur. If you slow down to, let's say, 50 miles per hour, everything comes into focus and you are better able to function and make better decisions. This is what meditation can do for you, it slows everything down and can give you clarity in your life. As many Jewish grandmothers have said in the kitchen throughout the centuries, TRY IT, YOU'LL LIKE IT!!!!

I now found myself living in a time warp, meaning time was just flying by once again. Always in the back of my mind was the thought that I was still waiting for the "Cities of Light" to appear. During this time I resumed traveling a lot, as well as reading. One day I was meditating and asked one of my Teachers why Anna (on a soul level) chose to go back to spirit. I was told she got tired and was given the option of continuing her spiritual work on the other side of the third dimensional Veil. The Veil refers to the human-created idea of separation from us and the higher dimensions of existence. I was also told that my services were still very much needed at the "Cities of Light." I gave reassurances that I was still ready, willing and able to do so.

At this time I continued to facilitate rebirthing and meditation classes. I enjoyed doing these because people really seemed to benefit from these gatherings. In addition, my Teachers and now Anna would always be present to support me and do the work.

The subject of karma and forgiveness would often come up for a lot of people during these sessions. Karma can be thought of as cause and effect. It can also be defined as "you reap what you sow." Karma is like gravity, you don't have to believe in it to be affected by it! Truth is, our thoughts, feelings, and actions act like boomerangs, so what you put out into the universe will eventually come back to you, good or bad, positive or negative. It is important to consciously guard your thoughts and feelings and make sure to never wish anyone harm, no matter what they may have done. Negative thoughts, emotions, and actions will eventually produce the same in your life. Conversely, sending out positive thoughts and feelings will attract the same into your life. If someone has deliberately hurt you, it is better to call on God to render "Divine Justice" than for you to wish them any harm. No one can escape the Law of Karma no matter how hard they try. If everyone understood how karma really works this would be a much kinder, gentler world for all of us to live in.

The power of forgiveness is another subject many people don't fully understand or are unable to put into practice. Remember, he or she who angers you controls you. We have all been hurt in our lives, as well as hurt others (intentionally or not). Forgiveness is one of the hardest things for us as humans to practice. It requires us to rise above our own pain, anger, pride, and everything in between. Try to think of a time in your life when you may have hurt someone, and then you were asking them to forgive you. Just because you forgive someone doesn't mean you still want or need them in your life, it just means you are able to cut your emotional connection to them. If you can do this, it can free you up and allow you to move forward in your life much more rapidly. I know circumstances can sometime be overwhelming for us and we cannot find the strength or will to forgive someone. In those cases I recommend you call in a Being of Light (of your choice) to help you. Get in the habit of asking for help from the "Company of Heaven" and just allow and receive what you are given.

Even though we can't control other people, we can learn to control how we react to them. How about the importance of forgiving ourselves? How often do we beat ourselves up for things we do or say on a daily basis? We all need to learn to be kinder to ourselves. After all, none of us are perfect no matter how hard we try to be. We all make mistakes and hopefully learn from them so as not to repeat them. If there are things you have done in your past, which hurt others or yourself, pray and ask for forgiveness first and then for the strength and wisdom not to repeat them. The more humble and sincere you are when asking for this, will help you get past it more rapidly.

Forgiving ourselves can be much more difficult for some people, but without doing it no one can ever really experience inner peace. If you need help, there are many avenues you can find. Please do not allow your human pride to block you from finding some guidance and assistance. If you would study the habits of happy successful people, you would learn they are never afraid to ask for help, and they rarely, if ever, make the same mistake twice. Good advice for all of us to follow, I believe.

St. Germain in his many books teaches the importance of paying attention. Where your attention rests is where you are. What your attention is focused on you become. When you place your attention on happy positive thoughts and things, it makes you happy, doesn't it? The reverse is also true. Try this out for yourself and you will see how powerful our attention really is. You may happen to know someone who walks through life with a perceived dark cloud always hanging over their head. They are always complaining at how everything bad always seems to happen to them. The truth is they are creating much if not all of this themselves, by their negative thoughts and feelings which are energetically drawing these things to them. All of us at some point in our lives have probably blamed others for our unhappiness and unpleasant circumstances. I was taught early on to stop blaming others and to accept full responsibility for my life. When you really start to do and feel this, you will feel much more empowered and in control of your life.

Many of us freely give away our energy/power to others without consciously even being aware of it. More times than not it involves those we are closest with such as family, friends, and people we work with. Pay attention to your energy the next time you are with somebody or have a phone conversation with someone. Are you more energized after this experience? Are you less energized after this experience?

If you want to take your energy/power back, you must first be conscious of the ways you give it away. Your energy drain can be to people, thoughts, feelings, and things. Some people thrive on taking other people's energy (usually due to their own deep seated fears and insecurities). I refer to these people as "Energy Vampires." Stop allowing people to do this to you, become more aware of the energy dynamics in all your personal relationships. When we allow others to take our energy, we feel depleted and exhausted, which can have a direct impact on one's self-esteem. Put an end to this now and take your power back. This is how part of us can take back complete responsibility for how we feel and act in our lives.

Remember, wherever your attention is, you are pouring your life energy there and inviting whatever that is into your life. So make a conscious effort to focus on positive people, places, and things and then you will draw them into your life and be happier. You cannot hang out with negative people and expect to live a positive, happy life. You know why it's hard to be happy? Because we refuse to let go of the things, thoughts, and people that make us feel less than or sad. Sometimes it is better to walk alone than with others heading in a negative wrong direction. It is very common for people on their spiritual journeys to drop friends and relationships which are no longer positive and nurturing. Don't be surprised if this happens to you.

It was now spring of 2012 and my friends at "Astara" (a place of spiritual teaching in California) invited me to facilitate a rebirthing workshop at a place call the "Integratron" near Joshua Tree, California. The Integratron is a geometric domed structure built over an intersection of powerful geomagnetic energy lines. If you are ever in this vicinity, it is well worth your time to visit and feel the powerful vortex of energy at this property and inside the dome.

I was excited as the group started arriving for the weekend events, as some of Anna's students from Durango, Colorado had registered to be here. I had not seen some of these people for many years and was looking forward to reconnecting with them, as they were like family.

Regardless of one's religious or spiritual background, training, practices and beliefs, at some point, somewhere and sometime, everyone has to face themselves in totality. This means to see the human imperfection which exists in all of us. In order for us to spiritually grow and advance we must either correct or release these things. Until we can break the patterns of our own imperfections and mistakes, we are not only bound to repeat them but also bound to the wheel of birth and rebirth.

No matter how spiritually evolved we are, or think we are, as long as we are residing in a third dimensional physical form (meaning we have not yet Ascended) there is more work for us to do on ourselves. Don't let your ego continue to fool you.

Ascension means our Souls have reached a higher level of spiritual consciousness and advancement and are no longer required to continue our training on planet Earth. (We are then no longer bound to the wheel of birth and rebirth in the third dimension.) We then permanently inhabit our new Energetic Light Body and function in the higher dimensions of reality.

In my experience, I find many people are afraid to look at the truth about themselves. Some are embarrassed, others feel guilt or shame at some of the things they have done or that have been done to them. There really is no way of getting around this if you wish to grow and move beyond one's own human imperfections and negative experiences. None of us are perfect, we all make mistakes and repeatedly come into a third dimensional human form in order to accelerate our learning process. We all have doubts, fears and insecurities we have acquired through our past and present lifetimes. It takes real courage and strength to look at one's self and see total truth. As I mentioned earlier in this book, if you are blessed enough to have someone in your life to help point out your flaws and weaknesses, your process can be greatly accelerated.

St. Germain teaches the way to free ourselves from self-imposed human limitations is by self-correction and self-control. (In other words, by being more conscious of our thoughts, feelings and actions at all times in our lives.)

The rebirthing process gives people the opportunity to release their emotional garbage (this was the term Anna used to describe past negative experiences, which we still carry with us that affect our lives). Once we can release these memories and negative energies, we are then lighter, freer and always happier.

The whole group had finally arrived at the "Integratron" and it was now time to begin the rebirthing. I explained to the group that the Teachers I primarily work with are Jesus, St. Germain, Archangel Michael, and Mother Mary, and not to be surprised if they see or feel their Presence and Energy during the rebirthing. I always give ALL the credit to these Amazing Beings of Light and Love for the work they do at these gatherings. I humbly do my small part to facilitate these workshops, but all Praise and Gratitude go to them and all the other Spiritual Beings who always show up and participate.

As the group began its deep breathing, the energy quickly increased in the dome as people began taking off into their own individual rebirthing experiences. Some people cry, some people laugh, some people sing or chant, while others just reach a blissful plateau. It is my job (kind of like a drill sergeant) to continue to coach and push people to keep breathing. The more one breathes, the higher levels of consciousness can be reached, which then maximizes their personal experience and healing. No two people in a group ever have the exact same experience, and no matter how many times you do this it will always be different as well. The uniqueness of the "Integratron" with its energy and perfect acoustics proved to be a very powerful venue.

During the rebirthing process as I was sitting in my chair, I could literally feel Anna's hands resting on my shoulders as she stood behind me. Her love and support are always a big part of the spiritual work that I continue to do to this day.

After the rebirthing, a couple of people came up to me and said they saw and felt Jesus working on them, as well as others around the room. I just smiled at them and quietly thanked Jesus for always supporting me and the work I do in any way he can. Another woman came up to me (who is a Native American Shaman and Healer in her own right) and was very excited because Mother Mary had spent a lot of time working with her that day. I always get a kick out of people when they share with me their spiritual experiences with these Magnificent Beings. I too can still remember how excited I was the first time I felt and experienced their Energy and Love.

The following morning I was asked to lead the group in a meditation. After the meditation Jesus delivered a message to the group and gave a special blessing to all in attendance. Before we broke as a group we all gave thanks to all the Higher Spiritual Beings and Teachers for all the energy and healing work we had received over the weekend.

Everyone seemed to enjoy their two-day "Integratron" experience, and it made me feel good to once again be of Service. On my long drive home to Arizona, I couldn't stop smiling because of how well the weekend turned out. Seeing the faces of people being worked on by the Teachers, and how happy this made them made my time and effort more than worth it. As proud as I am of my Teachers and all the Love and Support I receive from them, I could also feel how proud they were of me. That is a feeling I will never get tired of!

As 2012 continued, I was on the phone one day with a friend at Astara in California, and she told me about an energy-healing course called "Pranic Healing." They were hosting this event in a few weeks time and she invited me to attend. Initially I did not feel the urge to go do this and offered every excuse I could think of. The very next day I received their flyer in the mail promoting this event. As I began reading in detail what this course was teaching, I could feel the hair on the back of my neck stand up. Whenever this happens I know it is time for me to sit up and pay attention! I then asked St. Germain if I should go and take this class and he said "Absolutely!"

As a side note, I want to mention that Astara in California offers much in the way of spiritual teachings. The "Astara's Book of Life" lessons are some of the most powerful teachings you will find anywhere. If interested you can go to their website (astara.org) and get more information.

Pranic healing was developed by Grand Master Choa Kok Sui and involves techniques designed to cleanse and energize the physical body. I was always interested in healing due to my medical background, and after receiving St. Germain's strong endorsement, I looked forward to learning more about energy and its healing properties.

I had a few weeks before the course was to start and ordered some books ahead of time to read and familiarize myself with Pranic Healing. I learned that Pranic Healing was an energy-based healing method based on the management of the body's energy field.

I arrived at Astara for the two-day course and especially

since I did some reading beforehand, was excited to learn more about energy and how you can use it to heal. The course was taught by a dynamic young teacher by the name of Master Stephen Co. I learned his teacher Grand Master Choa Kok Sui was now back in spirit. Master Co was now teaching and carrying his beloved teacher's legacy forward. (I couldn't help but think in my small humble way, that I too was teaching and carrying Anna's legacy forward as well.)

I absolutely loved my experience at the level one introductory Pranic Healing course. Master Co is a tremendous teacher with a great sense of humor. I was immediately able to feel energy and found it easy to learn the many different healing techniques. Right after I finished this course I did some Pranic Healing work on my brother's painful knee, and the next day his pain was gone!

I was so motivated by these new energy techniques I had learned, that I spent the next six months traveling around the country taking more advanced classes. As I continued to learn more advanced methods and techniques, I found myself studying and reading even harder. I enjoyed learning how energy really works in our chakras (energy centers) which when congested or depleted due to negative energy, throw our bodies into a state of dis-ease and impending illness. It was interesting to note that negative emotions can have such a powerful affect not only on our mental health but also our physical health. When we hold on to negative emotions and experiences they block the normal flow of energy going through our bodies. This energy is necessary for us to maintain health and balance in our physical forms. Pranic Healing teaches how to remove these blockages and congestion which then allows the energy to once again flow freely and nourish our bodies.

This new information tied directly into the rebirthing work

I facilitate. During that process people have the opportunity to release their negative emotional obstructions as well. With my new found energy training, I could use this new knowledge to help further enhance peoples experiences during their own rebirthing process.

As I continued taking more advanced courses, I learned how powerful crystals can be when used correctly. All the new information I was being taught was so different and unique, compared to the traditional medicine and science I was trained in. Pranic Healing just seemed second nature to me and it was easy to grasp the concepts and to perform the techniques. I was able to prove for myself many times over, (by working on many different people) that "Pranic Healing" is a very powerful healing method.

I also took a course in Pranic psychotherapy which taught how to treat fears, phobias, addictions, and many other emotional issues many of us deal with on a day-to-day basis. This is an incredibly powerful way to help heal and transform people literally right before your eyes. I have seen, in my own experience, how a short ten minute energy session was able to change and transform someone in to a much more happier, positive person. Take my word for it, this Pranic Healing is powerful, effective, and in many cases you see immediate improvement in the people you are working on.

Do you remember earlier in this book when I was shown in a meditation that future healing will involve electron manipulation? I believe that Pranic energy healing does involve electron manipulation on some level. The simplicity of these powerful healing techniques are really amazing.

Master Co is truly a gifted teacher and healer in his own right. I am sure his mentor Grand Master Choa Kok Sui is very proud of the work he continues to do in his honor.

The underlying theme in Pranic Healing is that anyone and everyone can learn to do it. They also teach that once you learn to heal others you make sure to be of Service as often as you can. What good is having knowledge and skill to help others if you don't use them? I highly recommend this training for anyone interested in healing others and being of service. If you are interested in learning more about Pranic healing, their website is pranichealing.com.

I want to take a moment to thank St. Germain for strongly encouraging me to do this training. The new tools and techniques I have learned from Master Co have opened up more avenues in which I can now be of greater help and service to others. To Master Co I say thank you and "Atma Namaste."

As the years continued to fly by, it was now January of 2015 and a friend of mine mentioned that a lady he met from Sedona, Arizona wrote a book about the future "Cities of Light." Her name is Genii Townsend and her book is titled, *Something's Coming! Universal Cities of Light, Love, and Healing!* I was not familiar with her or the book at that time. Since I have been waiting for these Cities to appear, I knew this was a book I needed to read. (It was another one of those times where I could feel the hair stand up on the back of my neck.) I guess it's a good thing that I let my hair grow longer in the back of my head and neck, otherwise how would I know when I was supposed to go do something?

I got the book and finished reading it in a matter of days. I was totally taken in by the details and descriptions included about what these Cities will look like. After reading the book I felt re-energized and very optimistic about what was coming. I also knew I had to go travel up to Sedona and meet Genii face-to-face.

Our first meeting was like two old friends meeting up once again. There was a strong connection and feeling as if we had worked together before in another time and space. I initially went to Sedona to experience her Four Keys to Light Initiation class. She does this with the help of her many Spiritual Guides as well as her close friend Reverend Diana Runge. I enjoyed the Four Keys Initiation very much and felt a strong bond with all of them, including her business partner and friend Charles Betterton. I would strongly recommend if you have the chance to do this Initiation Class that you take full advantage of it. After a long weekend in Sedona, I returned home, happy for my new Sedona connections and friends.

A few days later I received an email from Genii saying her guides said I could be part of the City of Light in Sedona if I wished. They went on to say because of my medical background I would be taught the new healing technologies and would then be asked to teach these to the medical community. I checked with my Teachers and they said my connection to Genii and Sedona was no coincidence. They advised me to agree to do this if I chose to. (Remember, Free Will is always in play.)

I of course agreed to this, and cannot wait for my new job to start. If you are interested in learning more about the future "Cities of Light," Genii's book is a great place to start.

Chapter Twelve

Sole Currency vs. Soul Currency

I have shared with you much of my own personal and spiritual journey spanning the last thirty years. I want to share some more of what I have learned and some of the positive things we all have to look forward to.

Our Souls come into a physical embodiment lifetime after lifetime to learn, to grow, to experience, and to work out our karma. In some lifetimes we may be saints, in others not so much. It is all just part of our spiritual growth and evolution. Isn't it just as important to learn what not to do in life as it is what to do? By exercising our Free Will and making many mistakes along the way (as we all do) it allows us to learn at a much faster rate. I believe everyone who crosses our path in life serves as a teacher. Some teach by example the positive, right way to live, and others show us the exact opposite. Hopefully we use discernment in deciding what lessons to keep and which ones to discard. Each of our lifetimes is like a new movie. We are the actor, the director, the writer, and the producer. During our experience we are fully engaged in the third dimensional requirements and restrictions, which exist not only to test our physical survival, but our spiritual growth as well.

As soon as our lifetime/movie is completed, we shed our name, character, wardrobe, props, and script. We then get to review our performance with our Spiritual Guides and Teachers. Eventually we will then move on to another physical embodiment in order to continue our spiritual evolution.

After an infinite number of lifetimes, our Soul becomes advanced enough to graduate to the higher levels of learning and experience. This process is known as Ascension and is different for everyone in terms of timelines and experiences. It is important to note that after every lifetime we take the lessons learned, the love expressed, and the service performed in helping others with us in our Soul.

Over the years I have met many spiritual people on a similar type of journey as my own. Someone once referred to us as "Lightworkers." A loose definition of a "Lightworker" is someone who has dedicated their life to help raise the consciousness and awareness of humankind. This job is especially important at this time due to the important shifts currently taking place on our planet.

As I write, the whole planet's energy and vibration is being raised to lift all humanity. Each "Lightworker" has a specific role to play, as each one brings a different skill set and talent to the mix. Not sure if you are a "Lightworker"? If you care about others, respect and have compassion for others, you are indeed a "Lightworker" without even realizing it.

This brings me to another subject, being of service. What does this mean? What type of service are you supposed to do?

Being of service (at least in my mind) means being selfless in serving and helping others. It is very personal and individualized depending on your religious and spiritual beliefs, practices, and values. It is also influenced by your own current responsibilities, job, family . . . etc. True service means doing for others without expecting anything in return. There is an old saying, first cited in print in 1917 found over the doorway of a hospital in India, which reads, "SERVICE TO OTHERS IS THE RENT WE PAY FOR THE SPACE WE TAKE UP ON EARTH."

Being of service is different for each one of us, depending on our own life's mission, purpose and spiritual evolvement as well. Learn to practice doing random acts of kindness on a daily basis as one way of being of service. A great way to help raise the spirituality and consciousness of this planet is by showing more compassion to those of us less fortunate.

Changing the world one person at a time can be as simple as offering a smile, a word of encouragement or even a meal to someone in need. The love a parent gives to their child is also a way of being of service. You will have to decide for yourself what being of service means to you. All I know is that this world needs a lot more love, respect, compassion, acceptance of others different than ourselves, and more generosity in order for us all to move forward as one family. Any effort on your part to be of service is always appreciated by the "Company of Heaven," plus it causes your own Karmic Bank account to grow. (Just saying!)

This truly is an incredible time to be alive on this planet. Many different religious and spiritual disciplines are giving the same message of being in a time of great change. Just look around and see how fast our world is moving.

We are also in a time where the Ascended Masters are being allowed to send us all an incredible amount of Energy and Love. We ALL are receiving this much-needed help whether we are aware of it or not. Our Guides and Teachers are so loving, as they continue to help push us forward. They know how difficult life on planet Earth can be. Through their unconditional love, support, and yes, sometimes even their constructive criticism, they help us to grow and rise above the negativity currently engulfing this planet. We all have Spirit Guides and Angels assigned to us whether we know it our not, or even believe it or not. So why not start asking for their help, guidance and protection in your own life now!? They are here to help you, they have been assigned to help you, and it is up to you to ask for their assistance. (Remember, they must honor and respect the Law of Free Will.)

Have you ever heard the expression "the more you learn the more you realize you don't know?" That can certainly be applied to my spiritual quest for knowledge. I will never stop reading, studying, and learning anything I believe will make me a better person, and which allows me to be of greater service to others.

Who we are today is a sum total of all the decisions we have ever made. (both good and bad). Now is the perfect time to be conscious of all our decision-making and to be careful to always take the high road, so as not to create any negative karma for ourselves.

Now let's look at the future "Cities of Light," they will be a game changer for the planet and all its inhabitants. The God love, the God energy and the God vibrations and Sacred Tones will emanate from these Magnificent Cities, and once and for all bring permanent healing and peace to this great planet of ours.

I had a chance recently to meet some of our brave men and women military veterans, and was excited to share the news about the future healing technology with them.

I have been shown and told that the healing centers in these "Cities of Light" will be able to regrow arms, limbs, and any other body parts that were injured or lost either on the battlefield or in day-to-day life. In addition, there will be healing methods, which can literally wipe the brain clean of all traumatic and negative memories and experiences.

In speaking with these veterans and learning how devastating Post Traumatic Stress Disorder is to their lives,

I wanted to reassure them that help is on the way and not to give up. The new technology will be able to restore mind, body, and soul for all individuals and I cannot wait until we can do more, especially for these brave men and women.

Now if you recall, this book is divided into two parts, Sole Currency and Soul Currency. Part one of the book refers to my third dimensional existence and specifically "Sole Currency" which was money I earned when I was practicing Podiatric Medicine and Surgery. The play on the word "sole" refers to the bottom of the feet.

The second half of this book refers to "Soul Currency" and my spiritual journey, experiences, training, and lessons learned.

The absolute truth is the moment you take your last breath on planet Earth, everything you own now belongs to someone else. However, our spiritual development and who we really are will be ours forever as we go live in the higher realms of creation.

So what is Soul Currency? Where and how can I get some? Soul Currency is our Universal Supreme God working through us in a tangible way to help uplift humanity. You can also think of Soul currency as pure love, or good karma. You can earn Soul currency anywhere, by simply being of service and giving from your heart selflessly.

"Sole Currency", or third dimensional money, only has value on Earth. It has limited use and ownership, and you cannot take it with you when you leave.

"Soul Currency" is like your Spiritual Individual Retirement Account (I came up with the expression " Spiritual IRA"). It is multi-dimensional and represents God's Pure Love, Good Karma and is the Spiritual Currency you have earned over many lifetimes. It is infinite (unlike frequent flyer miles), and will never expire. On top of all this, you do get to take this with you when you leave. (How cool is that?)

So regardless of how old you are, or your past and present history, I would strongly suggest we all get busy Being of Service and earning some more "Soul Currency." I have dedicated the rest of my life to help anyone and everyone I can. Remember to always be humble and never forget where the real power in all things comes from. (The Universal Supreme God, which represents both masculine and feminine energies.)

My Spiritual Teachers and Guides are now pushing me harder than ever before to go out and teach, and do the work I have been trained to do. This command has also gone out to all "Lightworkers", as it is now time for the "collective consciousness of humankind" to be raised into the higher octaves of Peace and Love.

The reason for writing this book at this time is the hope that it will expose more people to the higher spiritual truths I have learned and humbly shared within these pages. In addition, I hope it opens more doors of opportunity in which to share the Amazing Love, Light, and Healing Energy of my Teachers. (I am in the habit of calling them my Teachers, when in fact they are ALL OUR TEACHERS.) My main focus and job will eventually be at the "Cites of Light." Until then I will continue to facilitate rebirthings, meditation classes, and do energy work and healing on as many people as I can.

I remember hearing a line from a movie which was "everything will be all right in the end, and if it's not, then trust me it's not yet the end!!" This is how I feel about our future here on Earth. I know there is a positive ending awaiting all of us. As I look back at the last thirty years of my life, all I can say is "what a long strange trip it's been!!" (Kudos to the Grateful Dead Band).

Dr. Rick Cohen

As I continue to wait for these magnificent "Cities of Light" to appear (hey, what's 30 years in human years anyway?), I can still hear Anna's voice saying, "IT WILL HAPPEN IN GOD'S TIME, NOT OURS!"

(Divine Timing, you gotta love it!)

UNTIL THEN, MAY THE UNIVERSAL SUPREME GOD CONTINUE TO BLESS US ALL!!!!!!!!!!!

The Fire-Walking Foot Doctor

Made in the USA
Columbia, SC
07 June 2023

17708004R00102